T0167135

CHRISTIANITY AND COSMIC CONSCIOUSNESS

A Commentary on the Words of Jesus

ALEXIS GEORG HOEN

TRUE DIRECTIONS
AN AFFILIATE OF TARCHER BOOKS

iUniverse®

CHRISTIANITY AND COSMIC CONSCIOUSNESS
A COMMENTARY ON THE WORDS OF JESUS

iUniverse books may be ordered through booksellers or by contacting:

iUniverse
1663 Liberty Drive
Bloomington, IN 47403
www.iuniverse.com
1-800-Authors (1-800-288-4677)

ISBN: 978-1-4917-5425-2 (sc)
ISBN: 978-1-4917-5424-5 (hc)
ISBN: 978-1-4917-5423-8 (e)

Library of Congress Control Number: 2014921368

Printed in the United States of America.

iUniverse rev. date: 2/3/2015

CONTENTS

PREFACE

In 1901, Canadian physician Richard Maurice Bucke published a book dealing with Cosmic Consciousness, the "mystic experience" of the common essence of the universe. In his book, Bucke documents the possession of such an experience by a number of individuals known to him, by several writers, and by virtually all creators of the world's great religions, including Jesus Christ.[1]

This implies that the words and acts of Jesus as reported to us in the Gospels are a guide not only to pleasing God or to being saved through forgiveness of sins but, above all, to living beyond oneself as an integral part of the cosmic whole.

It is important to elucidate this aspect of Christianity that has been neglected by the Christian churches. This problem has been highlighted by Matthew Fox, who says, "Christianity has been out of touch with its 'core,' its center, its sense of mystical practice and cosmic awareness."[2] Fox replaces the image of Jesus narrowly interpreted as payer for our individual sins with that of a cosmic Christ who "offers hope by insisting on the interconnectivity of all things and on the power of the human mind and spirit to experience personally this common glue among things."[3]

According to Jürgen Moltmann, "The modern discussion about cosmic christology ... was initiated in 1961 in a splendid and moving address by the Lutheran theologian Joseph Sittler at the General Assembly of the World Council of Churches in New Delhi. Sittler ... talked about the unity of the world, basing what he said on the cosmic Christ hymn in Col. 1:15–20. Christ is the foundation of all things, so that all things have access to his cosmic redemption."[4] According to Moltmann, cosmic christology is of particular practical importance at a time when man's preoccupation with himself threatens the very existence of the world so that "we must confront the 'threat to nature' with a 'christology of nature' in which the power of redemption does not stop short at the hearts of men and women and their morality, but extends to the whole of nature."[5] In 1995, the ecological implications of Christian teachings emphasizing the bond between man and his environment were reviewed by Denis Edwards, who writes, "The praxis of Christian discipleship involves the rediscovery of a new era in the Franciscan theology of companionship and family relationship between human beings and other creatures of the earth community."[6] We might safely change this quote to read "cosmic community." And Roger Haight in 1999, in his work reviewing Christianity as acceptable to "postmodern" thinking, said that "postmodernity involves Cosmic Consciousness."[7]

The Cosmic Consciousness referred to by these authors implies a realization of the bond between man and his cosmic environment and the responsibility arising therefrom. Christianity offers a way toward such a realization through Jesus's teaching and example.

The advance toward Cosmic Consciousness is the basis of many church rituals. Unfortunately, dogmatism obscures the cosmic significance of such rituals; the enormous importance of the Eucharist, for example, denoting the unity of God, the individual, and the community, is overshadowed by the argument of transubstantiation versus consubstantiation or transignification.[8] The latter term is appropriate because the *significance* of the event must not be overshadowed by whatever supernatural process some religious denominations believe it to involve, bewildering skeptics. The current work attempts to represent the core of Christian teaching without resorting to the supernatural and miraculous yet without trying to disprove it.

SECTION 1

Basic Concepts

Religion

The number of skeptics and atheists is growing in Western society, but even these individuals cannot avoid facing the basic significance of religion as such. Religion is a manifestation of spiritual hunger, as real and universal as physical hunger and thirst, a hunger arising from a quest for meaning in life and for life itself. Man wants to live beyond his individual limits, beyond his miserably short time on earth. "It is the infinite for which we hunger, and we ride gladly on every little wave that promises to bear us toward it."[9]

In his book *god is not Great,* Christopher Hitchens, while enumerating the evils attributable to religion, says that it will probably always be with us, as long as people are afraid of death.[10] One could paraphrase this statement in a more positive way and say that religion will be around as long there is a will to live.

The Universal Will to Live

The will to be, to exist, is universal. It is shared by all that exists down to the most elementary particles of matter, becoming conscious only in higher developed organisms. An atom, a molecule, and a rock have to have enough cohesiveness to resist the ever-present destructive forces that would keep them from what they want to be, and anything that is not programmed to exist perishes. In man that will becomes conscious, and the "knowledge of good and evil" brings with it the realization of mortality, an essential part of man's defenseless nakedness (Gn 3:7).

But if the "will to be," or, when applied to more developed beings, "the will to live" were nothing but a necessary quality adhering to all beings, they should be satisfied with the status quo. There must be a Creative Principle producing existence by causing matter-energy to form ever more complicated patterns that lie between the extremes of order and chaos, between stability and change. These extremes are brought into balance by the Creative Principle. If it were not present, the Big Bang would never have occurred and no ever-changing universe could have resulted. This Principle permeating the world is God in his or her most essential aspect. This concept of God does not involve a supreme being designing the world before it came into existence; rather it involves a Principle coexistent with the world. This view is elucidated by Alfred North Whitehead, who says, "It is as true to say that God creates the world, as that the world creates God ... both are in the grip of the ultimate metaphysical ground, the creative advance into novelty."[11] But that which is the "ultimate metaphysical ground of the world" must also be the ultimate metaphysical ground of its members. We are all representatives of the will to not only exist but to exist in an ever-developing mode. We all express consciously or unconsciously the creative force as our innermost essence: *we are the will to live.*

I am applying this term to all matter in the universe since life is only an extension of the all-pervading Creative Principle. Albert Schweitzer made a statement identical to the one above; he wrote, "I am life that wills to live, in the midst of life that wants to live."[12] He did not indicate, however, that that will to live or to exist extends to the most elementary particles of matter and energy, that it is the "ultimate metaphysical ground of the world." I believe that it is indeed the *ultimate ground* evidenced by the development of the universe. From here on I shall refer to it as the *Principle of Life* or *God.* Cosmic consciousness involves a comprehension of that Principle.

But dedication to life involves not only the development of ever more complex and efficient patterns but also their mutual support. And yet, Being per se can be manifested in multiple individual beings only to some limited extent, as they are competing with each other. My interests, to a large extent, are opposed to the interests and even to the existence of other people, objects, and resources. Even as a vegan, I have to destroy plants in order to eat, the space I occupy cannot be given to anyone else, the oxygen I consume is unavailable to other living beings, and sooner or later I shall come in conflict with somebody. No matter how hard the devout Jain, comically portrayed by Thomas Mann in his story "The Two Heads," may avoid hurting life, even to the point of sweeping the ground ahead of his steps in order not to hurt any small creatures, he cannot keep his white cells from mercilessly attacking any microscopic invaders. This necessary opposition to others is our "original sin" or, better said, our original dilemma of being *a part and apart* at the same time. It the paradox of serving the Principle of Life by partially opposing it.

Whether the Principle of Life is a conscious Supreme Being or the *elan vital* postulated by Henri Bergson,[13] a result of *Formative Causation* proposed by Rupert Sheldrake,[14] or simply an array of laws governing matter and energy as suggested by Stephen Hawking and Leonard Mlodinow in their popular book *The Grand Design*[15] does not matter in this context; all views point to *a God within all that exists.* Rene Dubos defines that indwelling God as "forces that create private worlds out of the universal stuff of the cosmos and thus enable life to express itself in countless individualities."[16]

The theosophist Alice Bailey (1880–1949) speaks of an "intelligent Will which controls, formulates, binds, constructs, develops and brings all to an ultimate perfection. This is that Will which is inherent in matter itself, and the tendency which is latent in the atom, in man, and in all that is,"[17] and she quotes the famous physicist John Tyndall as saying that the very atoms themselves seem to be "instinct with the desire for life."[18]

The idea of matter striving toward life first appeared in Western thought in the seventeenth century and was called "hylozoism" by its originator Ralph Cudworth.[19] Since it assumed a principle inherent in matter and did not consider matter as something directed by intent from the outside, it was thought by some to imply atheism, yet it is entirely compatible with *panentheism*, a belief in "the God within," in the striving of all matter toward a "creative advance into novelty." It does not, of course, insist on a conscious, deliberate advance, but it does not exclude it.

Conscious or not, the activity of that common Principle requires a connection, a communication between the participating elements of change that Whitehead calls the *principle of relativity*. He says "that the potentiality for being an element in a real concrescence of many entities into one actuality is the one general metaphysical character attaching to all entities, actual and non-actual, and that every item in its universe is involved in each concrescence. In other words it belongs to the nature of every 'being' that it is a potential for every 'becoming.' This is the 'principle of relativity.'"[20]

The common, "divine" essence of all existence makes it superfluous to ask for a purpose of life; we are, in our innermost nature, the carriers of life, and we cannot be but what we already are. If we were not carriers of life by nature, then the question of purpose of our life would lead to infinite regress; if the purpose of our lives is to serve God, what is the purpose of God? and so on. Similarly, we cannot ask for a purpose of the earth moving around the sun; it is simply obeying the laws inherent in the nature of the universe; these laws are its (unconscious) desires and the possibility of their fulfillment its "freedom."

Once we realize that the will to live constitutes our innermost nature, our foremost desire, we shall be unable to agree with Stephen Weinberg, who says that "the more the universe seems comprehensible, the more it also seems pointless."[21] For even though the universe may someday end and disappear without a trace, having existed within that universe will mean we have fulfilled our essential want. In the words of Pierre Teilhard de Chardin, "if progress is a myth, that is to say, if faced with the work involved we can say: 'What is the good of it all?' our efforts flag. With that the whole of evolution will come to a halt because *we are evolution*"[22] (italics in the original French text).

The insight that our innermost nature, the will to live, is identical with the innermost nature of the entire creation is expressed in the ancient Hindu belief that Atman, our highest or deepest Self,[23] is identical to the essence of the universe, an essence that can be conceived either as pure potential Being, Nirguna Brahman, or realized Being manifesting itself in the creative process of which certain qualities can be predicated, Saguna Brahman.[24] In terms of Whitehead's philosophy, the first concept may be related to the primordial nature of God,[25] the latter to his consequent nature.[26] Our identity with this active Principle is expressed by the well-known statement *"that art thou"* in the Chandogya Upanishad. Contrary to a common opinion, that should not be taken to mean that the structures of this world are somehow unreal, being figments of our imagination; it means that these structures are identical to us and to each other in their innermost being, the will to reality, to life and form, a will that manifests itself in their diversity. "That is the finest essence—the whole world has that as its soul. That is Reality (*satya*). That is Atman (Soul). That art thou, Svetaketu."[27] The existence of an ultimate reality, Brahman, does not render the reality that we perceive with our senses illusory. If indeed *everything* is an illusion, then there is no difference between the real world and the imagined world. The term *illusion* has meaning only if it denotes an erroneous perception (such as a dream) among valid ones.

Immortality

Since my innermost nature is identical to that of the plenum of existence, it will persist for the duration of time. Reduced to that superpersonal entity, I am immortal. Ludwig Feuerbach, writing on death and immortality in 1830, observed, "your essence remains after your death"[28] and later, in the same work, "as a living being you exist in infinite life itself."[29]

Friedrich Schleiermacher, thirty-one years earlier, speaking about religion and our yearning for the infinite, put it thus:

> What concerns immortality, I am compelled to say, the way most people view it and their craving for it, is quite irreligious, diametrically opposed to the spirit of religion, their desire has no other foundation except the inclination against that which is the goal of religion. Remember, that all within it strives to widen the sharply defined limits of our personality, so that they gradually lose themselves in the infinite, that by contemplating the Universe we become as far as possible one with it; but they resist the Infinite, they do not want to get out of their limits, they do

not want to be anything but themselves and they are anxiously concerned with their individuality ... In the midst of the finite to become one with the Infinite and to experience eternity in a moment of time, that is the immortality of religion.[30]

The Experience of Oneness

The above considerations are not intended to, nor can they, disprove some sort of individual life after death. Rather they point beyond it, toward survival of our innermost nature, of something that matters most, the immortal Principle of Life. The recognition of that essential Principle within us and within all that exists may be referred to as *Self-realization*. The word *Self,* denoting our common innermost nature, is capitalized, as opposed to the narrowly conceived "selfish" self.

Paramahansa Yogananda, the Hindu theologian and founder of the Self-Realization Fellowship, defines Self-realization as "the knowing—in body mind and soul—*that we are one with the omnipresence of God,* that we do not have to pray that it come to us, that we are not merely near it at all times, but that God's omnipresence is our omnipresence; that we are just as much part of Him as we ever will be. All we have to do is improve our knowing."[31]

But it is not only *knowing* that is involved here. The word *realize* has two meanings in the English language. To realize means first "to comprehend" and second "to make real through action." *Self-realization* then means not only comprehension of Self but also acting in accordance with that insight which, as I shall demonstrate, involves following moral laws. At this juncture, however, we are primarily concerned with the *knowing*. *Because of the identity of the innermost nature of all that exists, the knowing must necessarily lead to Cosmic Consciousness.*

Philosophical speculation about the omnipresence of the One uniting the many goes back to Parmenides, born 515 BCE. In a poem translated into English in 1892 by John Bennet, Parmenides says, "One path is left for us only to speak of, namely that *It is*. In it are very many tokens that what is is uncreated and indestructible, alone, complete, immovable and without end. Nor was it ever, nor will it be; for now *it is*, all at once, a continuous one."[32] Such a vision does not contradict the creative advance into novelty as long as we see such an advance as an essential manifestation of "the one" timeless Being.

Actually "experiencing" the One, which is usually referred to as mysticism, has been claimed by Plotinus, who reports that it occurred to him personally four times. Plotinus's successors, the Neoplatonists, carried on the idea of the One in a philosophic fashion with involvement of theurgic magic in the case of Iamblichus, who also postulated the existence of two Ones, one completely transcendent, the other the source of all creation,[33] echoes of Nirguna and Saguna Brahman in Hinduism,[24] foreshadowing Meister Eckhart's concepts of Godhead and God when he says that God and Godhead differ by acting and not acting,[34] and Whitehead's primordial and consequent nature of God.[25,26] *Tao Te Ching*, the "authoritative book" on the Tao (the Way, the basis of Taoism) describes the One as a Principle holding the world together: "the myriad creatures in virtue of the One are alive."[35]

There are numerous studies dealing with the One indwelling principle uniting the many,[36,37] including one enlarging upon the vision of Teilhard de Chardin[38] to which I shall refer shortly.

Louise Nelstrop and others have reviewed "Christian mysticism" in a thoroughly comprehensive book,[39] but reading some of these philosophical accounts, including the well-known book by William James,[40] one has the impression of students of human behavior looking in from the outside, not being privy to "knowing" by personal experience. Such "knowing" may come to us as a sudden revelation in various degrees of intensity as described by Bucke.[41]

As I walk along a street and see the setting sun illuminate a green lawn on which two dogs are playing, and as I hear birds chirping in a tree, I realize that the sun, the warm breeze, the grass, the dogs, the birds, and I are all part and parcel of a life-giving force. Moreover, I realize that eons of cataclysms in immeasurable space, countless collisions, explosions, and violent transformations have taken place to produce this earth, this moment, this life of mine. And my life is connected with countless other lives, countless events taking place around it, in ever-widening circles, even to the end of the universe. This universe nourishes me and maintains me with air to breathe, with light to see, with love to exchange. It will eventually absorb my mortal remains and all that I have done and produced with all its good and bad effects on my contemporaries and on future generations. Life itself will go on, mortal in all its manifestations, immortal in essence.

As I walk on, a small dry leaf flutters and falls on the pavement in front of me. I am not superior to that leaf either in the longer duration of my life or in the size of my body when these parameters are considered relative to the duration or the size of the universe, and even though I represent a much higher state of evolution than the leaf, in relation to the huge plenum of Being constituting the universe, my own contribution is as infinitesimal as that of the leaf.

Of course, any creature, including myself, values things on a scale of their importance for its survival. To a dog, a bone is more important than a rose. All the rose cares about are nutrients in the soil, water, and light. And if there were some small creature—a snail, perhaps, or a bacterium—subsisting on dry leaves, the aforementioned leaf would be for it the most precious thing in the world. But these are relative values depending on the kind of creature one is. They all fade before the one absolute value: the contribution to life, common to all.

As a human being, I am superior to other creatures in one way: my ability to understand the universal principle of life, the ability to value things in relation to that principle, apart from their possible individual importance for myself, and the realization of my quantitative insignificance related to the immensity of the universe. Yet that immensity of Creative Being has narrowed down to produce my little world and my person, to whom it has lent its own essence and an awareness thereof. If I believe in a personal, conscious God, then I can also believe that I was created in God's image and likeness not only because I share his essential will toward creative novelty but also because of the realization of that will in thought and deed. If, however, I do not believe in such a conscious creator, then my own Cosmic Consciousness is simply the apotheosis of the universal will to live, the acme of its development. In any event I am the *product*, the *knower*, and the *actor* of the Principle of Life.

Teilhard de Chardin defines this relationship in the following way: "In truth, I doubt that there is for a thinking being a more decisive moment than that when the scales drop from his eyes and he realizes that he is not an element lost in a cosmic waste, but that there is a universal will to life which converges and humanizes itself in him."[42] This is another statement implying that such a realization allows me to find life, according to my innermost essence, outside my own individual existence, apart from any possible individual life after death. It is the "Infinite," the entity comprising all limited entities, that I have grasped.

Jeffery Long describes the phenomenon of Moksha—that is, liberation, in the Hindu religion, which entails life through unity with the divine, "a true understanding of the interdependence of all beings, including their mutual implication with divine existence, a conscious participation in the divine creative process,"[43] and Buddhist thought produces the same insight as can be seen in this excerpt from Sam Tchen Kham Pa (Dayalshanti Ghose):

> Abide in This
> Live only in This
> Be self-effacing
> And may your soul shine with Its Infinite Light, Its
> supreme peace,
> O sublime immortality, I am ever in Thee
> I am no longer distinct from Thee ... [44]

But the "sublime immortality" has a meaning only as a final satisfaction of my will to be, called here the will to live, fulfilled by stepping beyond my individual being and yet accepting it as a contribution to being in general. I have to transcend my individuality rather than escape from it, the latter apparently Schopenhauer's goal, often thought to be also that of Buddhism. It is important for the purpose of this book to understand that Christianity challenges us to accept life as it is, even with its adversity, as pointed out by Paul Tillich, who writes, "In Christianity the demand is made to accept suffering as an element of finitude with an ultimate courage and thereby overcome that suffering which is dependent on existential estrangement, which is mere destruction."[45] *Existential estrangement* denotes suffering seen purely as a threat to one's existence without a redeeming value. The German version simply says, "Christianity demands that one courageously accepts suffering as an element of our finitude and approves of the finitude despite the suffering which it entails."[46] This acceptance of whatever happens, this *amor fati,* does not denote viewing suffering as something good, but rather accepting it as a necessary ingredient and challenge within the goodness of life.

Gradual Self-realization

The fact that our Self-fulfillment lies in the dedication to creation as a whole implies the need to love our fellow creatures. It is indeed possible to experience Cosmic Consciousness as a momentary realization of one's unity with the Creative Principle, but leaving others behind as one enjoys a blissful state contradicts that very Principle. Therefore there is a self-defeating element in this withdrawal from ordinary life in order to realize my part in universal life. Only by caring for other individuals, rather than enclosing them as an abstract entity into the totality of our universe, by living for and through others, can most of us *gradually realize* our identity with the Creative Principle, the Principle of Life.

The Hindu theologian Maharishi Mahesh Yogi designed a method to "contact Being"—that is, to experience Cosmic Consciousness by the process of Transcendental Meditation.[47] According to Maharishi, touching the ground of Being through his technique improves one's loving relationship with others and the world,[48] and he thus connects the brief moments of enlightenment with our daily life and our interaction with others. This improvement of our fitting in with our environment is an important benefit of Transcendental Meditation, much more important than the improvement of physical health allegedly connected with it.[49]

Self-realization, which, by revealing to us our common innermost nature reveals our identity with others, is the basis for our moral and ethical principles. This is expressed by the view that God, the Creator, in his most basic concept the Principle of Life, is also the giver of the moral laws. Thus, Rudolph Bultmann writes, "God encounters man directly in the *nomos*, the law of the Old Testament the purpose of which is no other than to lead man to life."[50] And since this God dwells within us, these moral laws are a way to our Self-fulfillment. Man is created in the image and likeness of God (Gn 1:27); therefore, man's innermost will is the same as the will of God. Meister Eckhart puts it this way: "One should not conceive and view God as outside of oneself, but as one's own and as that which is within oneself; moreover one should not serve and act for the sake of some Why, neither for the sake of God, nor for one's own honor, nor for whatever may be outside of oneself, but only for the sake of that which is one's own being and one's own life within."[51]

Tillich makes a similar statement about theonomy, the law of God, when he says, "Theonomy does not mean the acceptance of a divine law imposed on reason by the highest authority; it means autonomous reason united with its own depth."[52] And Bultmann says, "Radical obedience is only possible when a man understands the demand and affirms it from within himself."[53]

In 1876, F. H. Bradley wrote, "The good self satisfies us because it answers to our real being. It is a harmony, it is subordinated into a system; and thus, in taking its content into our wills and realizing that, we feel that we realize ourselves as the true infinite, as one permanent harmonious whole."[54]

Viktor Frankl addresses the close connection between Self-realization and caring for others in his book *Man's Search for Ultimate*

Meaning. He writes, "Thus human existence—at least as long as it is not neurotically distorted—is always directed at something, or someone, other than itself, be it meaning to fulfill or another human being to encounter lovingly. I have termed this constitutive characteristic of human existence 'self-transcendence.' What is called 'Self-actualization' is ultimately, in effect, the unintentional by-product of self-transcendence."[55]

The step-by-step realization of our divine essence through attitude and moral action is open to everyone, whereas sudden enlightenment, be it spontaneous or achieved through meditation, remains reserved for only a few and cannot last because of our unavoidable conflicts with others, our original fault. Through morality and love, I approach the ultimate goal of my innermost nature by minimizing my opposition to whatever presents itself to me. Whereas the attainment of Cosmic Consciousness or Self-realization can be compared to a comprehensive view from a tower, my life with that vision as a goal compares to ascending the steps leading to the top. The essential statements of Jesus, to be discussed in this book, lead us toward such a step-by-step approach to Cosmic Consciousness through progressive realization of our identity with the Principle of Life.

We find the scriptural statement connecting our innermost nature, the God within us, with service to others in Mark 12:30–31, where quotes from Deuteronomy 6:5 and Leviticus 19:18 are combined: "You shall love the Lord your God with all your heart, with all your soul, with all your mind and with all your strength," and "you shall love your neighbor as yourself." We cannot love God, the Principle of Life, without loving and serving his manifestation, his creatures, especially those nearest to us.

In the Buddhist religion, the individual egotistic enlightenment, *arhatship*, which permits one to attain nirvana, is counterbalanced by the Bodhisattva doctrine. The path of arhatship "deprived the world of the holy men and women who had attained *nirvana* and passed away. A *bodhisattva* was defined as one who strove to gain *bodhi* (enlightenment) and scorned such *nirvana*, as he wished to help and succor his fellow creatures in the world of sorrow, sin and impermanence."[56]

Love

We are primarily concerned with the concepts of the Christian religion, and must look deeper into the meaning of the word *love* in the Judeo-Christian scriptures. Many comments are made about the different connotations of that word, which in the ancient Greek is designated by a number of varying terms, depending on its particular application. Yet we speak in the same breath of loving God as we speak of loving our neighbor. It appears that the biblical Hebrew word for *love* (*ahava*), which would have been quoted by Jesus, is the same whether applied to God or a human person, thus very much corresponding to our concept of "love."

The idea of loving God may be puzzling; it seems that one has to imagine him as a benevolent person to have any sort of emotion directed toward him—to actually substitute the image of a parent or a close friend for that of God. But if God in his essence is life, and life is my supreme good, then that realization should denote love, in this case meaning unconditional attachment through identity in essence and purpose.

In the context of "love your neighbor as yourself" the word *love* implies a feeling that reaches deeper than sexual attraction, family ties, or friendship—love that has no selfish motive, although it may be occasioned by it. Such love implies identification; I hurt when my neighbor hurts, and I rejoice when he or she is happy. The identification begins with people closest to me but, with only a little imagination, will extend to other creatures, to our environment, and finally to the totality of creation. I feel compassion for animals, I am hurt by man's brutality toward his environment, and I rejoice in the manifestations of nature surrounding me.

Can "loving the forest" mean that I identify with it, in addition to enjoying fresh air and peace? Yes, because I perceive in it the pulse of life, our common good, the preservation of which I value as if it were my own.

Progressive identification has been called "the ordering of love."[57,58] It can never reach completion, not even among humans, because of the unavoidable opposition between individuals and because we all differ in many respects. Yet we all share our innermost nature, the will to live, some manifestations of which may be the same and some that may be different. Tillich defines this situation correctly when he says, "The acceptance of another self by participating in his personal center is the core of love in the sense of *agape*, the New Testament term."[59] This common personal center is the very "God Within,"[16] the Principle of Life we all share.

How can I love my enemies, bless those who curse me, and pray for those who mistreat me (Lk 6:28)? Not only by trying to understand their actions but, above all, by realizing that we are the same in our innermost nature, however misguided and distorted it may become, by "participating in their personal center."

The Human Person

We find the concept of a common innermost nature in the writings of the twelfth-century Chinese sage Chu Hsi—also known as Zhu Xi—who postulated a universally indwelling Principle *li* surrounded by the "psycho-physical stuff" he referred to as *chi*.[60] If there is a soul surviving our body after death, it must be part of that "psycho-physical stuff," for it is different for every person. While we are alive, our innermost nature, the will to live, acts through the "psycho-physical stuff" on three different levels that always coexist and that I shall call the *id,* the *ego,* and the *superego,* not in exact conformance with the current definition of these terms by psychologists. These levels find their expression in our attitudes toward our environment.

The *id* cares only about its individual survival and is devoted only to itself. The thief, the murderer, and two hungry creatures fighting for a piece of bread consider nothing but their self-interest.

The *ego* moves a step further by realizing that survival involves compromise. It takes others into consideration in order to help itself, and it loves those who support it. It is possible to explain many laws and habits inherent in an organized society by just such egoism of its members, a "tit-for-tat" behavior. B. F. Skinner, an exponent of "behaviorism," writes, "The way one person treats another is determined by reciprocal action … We refrain from hurting others, not because we 'know how it feels to be hurt,' but 1) because hurting other members of the species reduces the chances that the species will survive, and 2) when we have hurt others we ourselves have been hurt."[61]

It is not clear why I would try to help an animal in pain if my only motive in treating other creatures is the consideration of reciprocity and the genetically inherited loyalty to my species. I suppose Skinner would say that taking pity on an animal is caused by transference of a pattern of moral action learned within the structure of society, and indeed such an application of egotistic motives is imaginable. And yet it seems to me that progressive identification with others leading to life outside our individual limits offers a more unified explanation of human endeavors. It explains not only our concern for others but also Skinner's own search for the basis of human behavior and his desire to share it with others. It explains the artist's desire to capture the essence of the world, and the scientist's quest for discovery.

This realization of unity with all other creatures and the subservience of our actions to that principle is a function of the *superego*. Of course, any action requires motivation, so that in living through others, and ultimately realizing our unity with the universe, we satisfy our personal desire to live. But here the contrast between egoism and altruism becomes meaningless; the two concepts merge in the concept of "superegoism." The identification with others ceases to be a matter of convenience and becomes a life-giving communion, and that applies not only to morals but also to man's achievements in science, art, and even technology. According to Einstein "the whole purpose of science and art is to awaken the cosmic religious feeling."[62]

All the three attitudes described above do not necessarily depend on consciousness. Just as I adjust my balance without thinking when I stumble over an obstacle, I can act spontaneously even on the third level described above. I can sacrifice myself for another person on the spur of the moment, certainly without considering the moral, and therefore cosmic, significance of my action. People have jumped into burning houses to rescue someone else without giving any thought to what they were doing. Yet I may be aware on any of the three levels, and I need consciousness for a full realization of my innermost nature. This additional element of my personality mediating between *li* and *chi* is addressed in a remarkable passage in the apocryphal gospel of Mary Magdalene. It reads as follows: "'Lord, if someone meets you in a moment of vision, is it through the soul [*psyche*] that they see or is it through the Spirit [*Pneuma*]?' The Teacher answered: 'It is neither through the soul nor the spirit, but the *nous* between the two which sees the vision and it is this which ... '"[63] The remainder of the sentence is lost with the missing pages of the ancient document. We must assume that "meeting Jesus" means grasping his truth.

The translator inserted Greek words into the Coptic text. We can safely assume that Jesus and Mary Magdalene did not converse either in Greek or Coptic. If they really said what is quoted here, they must have used Aramaic words based on Hebrew religious concepts. *Psyche* may well be an imperfect translation of the Hebrew *nephesh* identified with the individual life of a person that ceases to exist after death[64] (the *anima vegetativa*). The Hebrew word for *spirit* is *Ruah*, which is related to emotion and mentality (*anima animalis*) and not necessarily to a divine element, the latter referred to as *Chaya* or *Life*. This is what I understand to be the spirit of God as well as the innermost nature of all that exists. There is also the concept of *Neshamah*, which "represents the deepest intuitive power which leads to the secrets of God and the universe."[65,66] This may well correspond to the Greek *nous*. It must be remembered that all these concepts

31

were reinterpreted by the Jewish mystics many centuries after Jesus, so attributing their use to him must remain questionable. Still, they are applicable in the framework of this book.

It is interesting to note that according to Chu Hsi, "it is the responsibility of the mind to realize the good nature with which one is born."[67] The closest Greek translation of *mind* is *nous,* an interesting parallel to the gospel of Mary Magdalene.

Freedom and the Existence of Evil

If the will to live and to serve life is our core, our innermost nature, then "freedom" is the unobstructed way toward fulfillment of that nature, not the alleged "free will" denoting the possibility of deciding between good and evil. Such a choice is not possible, because it was already made for us at the moment we came into being. In accordance with our innermost nature, we constantly seek the best possible service to life and the most perfect degree of love and service to others, but we are constantly impeded by adverse circumstances, by temptation and error. The innermost human nature is like a beam of light moving forward in accordance with its essence, deflected by the obstacles it encounters and slowed down by the media through which it passes. It may well be that whereas we are not "free" to decide between good and evil in its basic forms, we have the so-called freedom of the will to choose the best course to do so. In that case, some obstacles are caused by external circumstances, some by freely chosen erroneous attitudes.

The view that by virtue of our innermost nature we are compelled to want the good, that we cannot deviate from the path of "creative advance into novelty" by supporting all positive change, by loving other beings as exponents of that advance, is supported by the statement that man is created in the image and likeness of God (Gn 1:26). For God, believed in as a conscious agent, is also free to respond to circumstances and to make decisions, but is not free to deviate from his own goodness.

If the basic freedom we desire is the fulfillment of our innermost nature, then Jesus's statement "the truth will set you free" (Jn 8:32) means that the truth as he taught it shows us the least encumbered way to strive toward such fulfillment. We can again refer to the gospel of Mary Magdalene that describes the "ascent" of the soul toward "freedom from ignorance."[68]

Our goal then is to achieve the best possible equilibrium between all the "psycho-physical stuffs" surrounding us and our own, a task realized by the superego, achievable only in an asymptotic fashion. The obstacles to our Self-realization coming from within and from without are necessary; without them there would be no life, no effort, no gradation of value. Without failure there would be no success; without pain there would be no joy. Continued creative activity in which we participate requires death, for the old has to be replaced by the new. The Principle of Life is a principle of change. How does the goodness of the Creator fit into this concept?

It is appropriate in this context to recall the Kabbalistic concept of Tsimtsum,[69] the withdrawal of God from a portion of his plenum to make room for the world. We might expand this concept to involve partial withdrawal of pure Being to make room for not-being, to allow for continuous creation giving rise to new forms that supersede old ones, to allow for destruction for the sake of novelty, for darkness to give meaning to light. Thus Lucifer, the Prince of Darkness, becomes the "bringer of light" to the world. The One becomes many, and the plenum of life is parceled out into unities that are limited in time and space.

Such a view presupposes the immanence of God, the Creative Principle, in the world, but it does not imply pantheism. God is indeed present in all things and all events, but only as their positive aspect. The destruction of Hiroshima by the atom bomb was a manifestation of Satan, but the opportunity it presented for rebuilding, for people's mutual assistance, even perhaps for maintaining peace in the future, and the resulting good uses of nuclear power—all these things are the manifestation of God. In the duration of my own life, I die every moment and I am born anew. The constructive power of good causes the latter, and the destructive power of evil has caused the former. Here is a quote from Jacob Boehme:

> There are in all creatures of this world a good and an evil will and production; in men, in animals, birds, fish, worms, as well as in everything that exists; in gold, in silver, tin, copper, iron, steel, wood, vegetables, leaves and grass, as well as in the earth, in stones, in water, and in all that one can investigate. There is nothing in nature without good and evil inside of it, everything moves and lives in this twofold drive, whatever it may be.[70]

The Taoist belief in the pervasive coexistence of yin and yang, one being the principle of darkness, the other one that of light, has a similar connotation.[71]

The Greek Stoic philosopher, Chrysippus recognized the mutual dependence of good and evil in the third century BC.[72] One cannot completely agree with his statement "that good cannot *exist* without the existence of evil" if *existence* means *Being* and if we identify good with the ground of Being, with God, because by definition, Being *is*, but we can maintain that God, the epitome of good, *is dependent on evil for his manifestation,* on that *withdrawal* from the plenum of pure Being. Here again we might see the difference between Nirguna Brahman and Saguna Brahman, only the latter needing the opposition of evil, and Meister Eckhart's Godhead and God, differing by simply being in the former case and acting—that is, manifesting himself, in the latter.[34]

The dependence of the manifestation of good on the existence of evil is a situation we perceive based on observation and logic. Some people experience a view of the world devoid of evil, "that all things work together for the good of each and all,"[73] including one known to me personally.[74] Such an experience transcends rational thinking and is not necessarily required for an interpretation of Christianity herein proposed. Many devout individuals also believe that all evil is somehow compensated for by a caring God, if not in this world, then in the next, but such a belief, even if it is correct, requires pure faith unfounded on what is observed.

Personification of God

So far we have only established the existence of a Creative Principle with which we can identify and achieve eternal life or, better said, timelessness through love of the world and of other beings and by opposing the destructive forces of evil. It is my contention that the acceptance of Jesus as our Savior can be deduced from the correspondence of our innermost nature, revealed to us by him, to that of God viewed purely as an all-pervading Creative Principle. Other attributes ascribed to God by the tradition of the Church do not contradict that view. Yet if God is not conceived first and foremost as a Creative Principle, the belief in him loses its rational basis and becomes a matter of faith.

Still, most of us, no matter how devoted to the Creative Principle, no matter how aware of our unity with it, would feel closer to a conscious person with whom we could identify, whom we could love, since we are conscious people ourselves.

As long as the phenomenon of consciousness has not been explained, we cannot know whether that phenomenon results from the progressive evolution of the animal nervous system, or whether it permeates all beings, animate or inanimate, not realized until the nervous system has reached a certain stage of development. Theistic and, for that matter deistic, thinking assumes consciousness preexisting creation; "In the beginning was the Word" (Jn 1:1).

But once popular thinking accepts the existence of a conscious person who is creator of all and superior to all, it endows that person with the features of a superior ruler, a king of kings who metes out reward and punishment to his subjects, practicing perfect justice and superior mercy, who responds to petitions as long as they are of benefit to the petitioner, a legislator who has established the laws of nature. The three concepts of God—first as a Creative Principle, second as a conscious person, third as a benevolent ruler—do not contradict one another; the first, I believe, is self-evident, and the other two require faith, perhaps revelation and grace, and perhaps a "God gene," postulated by Dean Hamer. In his book Hamer says, "I believe that our genetic predisposition for faith is no accident. It provides us with a sense of purpose beyond ourselves and keeps us from being incapacitated by our dread of mortality."[75]

But seeking a "purpose beyond ourselves" is not limited to people looking toward a personal God and an afterlife. It is characteristic of everyone's search of life beyond individual limits here and now. This has already been illustrated by a quote from Victor Frankl's book: "Human existence … is always directed at something or someone other than itself."[55] Thus, by transcending himself or herself, even the atheist communes with universal existence, the Principle of Life, the impersonal God at the very least.

Meister Eckhart, who reaches for the very ground of Being, even beyond its creative manifestation, says, "Therefore we pray to God, that we may get rid of 'God,' and that we grasp and eternally enjoy the truth there where the highest angels and the fly and the soul are equal, there where I stood and wanted to be what I was and was what I wanted to be."[76] In the process of Self-realization it is necessary that we grasp our identity with the Principle of Life, the essence of God, without adding to his image all the monarchical qualities claimed by the Church. *Still, we may believe in those qualities as long as we do not forget that God is first and foremost the Creative Principle of Life that also constitutes and defines our innermost nature.*

The Message of Jesus

Based on the foregoing considerations, the New Testament can be read in different ways in conformity with different, more or less rational attitudes. At one extreme it may be taken as an account, imbued with myth, expressing, in a number of symbols and teachings, our need and our ability to dedicate ourselves to the Principle of Life. At the other extreme, we may view it as an account of historically validated miracles and teachings leading us to God, a loving father and ruler. The first interpretation would lend a not usually perceived meaning to the statement "blessed are those who have not seen and have believed" (Jn 20:29). It might mean that one is blessed if one recognizes the spiritual truth of the Gospels regardless of their historic accuracy. Fyodor Dostoyevsky puts it thus: "If anyone could prove to me that Christ is outside the truth, and if the truth really did exclude Christ, I should prefer to stay with Christ and not with truth."[77] No doubt, he is saying that he would choose spiritual truth over historical facticity.

In the quest for the historical Jesus, great efforts have been made to determine which of the sayings attributed to him in the Gospels are genuinely his.[78] I believe that we have to accept the message of the Gospels as that of Jesus because his words as reported there show great consistency in purpose and meaning and because it is impossible to prove what other message, if any, Jesus may have intended to convey. And yet, any distillation of the truth of a text, as one sees it, must involve attributing a lesser significance to some of the quotes or even rejecting them altogether.

The letter of James, the brother of Jesus, appointed by him, according to the gospel of Thomas, as his successor[79] relates Jesus's teaching much as the Gospels do, and the Didache, a book containing instructions for the early Christian community,[80] does the same. But, according to the introduction to the letter of James in the New American Bible, even that authorship is in doubt, and the Didache may not be as early a document as some authors think, and therefore not necessarily a fresh account of what Jesus said. Thus Jesus's actual words remain uncertain, and I think that Matthew Fox is right when he says that the concept of the historical Jesus must be balanced by that of the cosmic Christ,[81] the proclaimer of the truth emerging to us from the Gospels. But that very truth of the Gospels justifies the statement that "the farmer's wife who believes in the Immaculate Conception of the Holy Mary, in the Dear Lord, and all the Saints still has come closer to the truth than the behaviorist."[82]

Feuerbach believed that our entire concept of God is a projection of human qualities into a superior Being.[83] Such *projection* would apply to a personal God, patterned after the features of a terrestrial ruler. But believing in our unity with the Principle of Life is not a matter of *projection* but of *realization*, first in the sense of comprehension and second in the sense of putting into action. The Gospels indeed contain much of the projection of human qualities onto God. Yet by the basic challenge to love God and to love one's neighbor, they offer to us the most direct way to comprehend the Creative Principle constituting our innermost nature and uniting us to the universe. *This realization of unity is Cosmic Consciousness.*

To achieve it we do not have to endow the Creative Principle of Life with features of a benevolent, omniscient monarch, but neither do we have to reject the naive views of the farmer's wife mentioned earlier.

My views on the important problem of the divinity of Jesus are contained in the comments concerning the Sixth Word from the cross, "It is finished," and those on the "kingdom of heaven" in the section on the first beatitude.

SECTION 2

The Seven Last Words

The Seven Last Words spoken by Jesus from the cross are those of a dying human being in strict conformance with the teachings he pronounced before his final hours. They open the door to considerations essential for the realization of our unity with the Creative Principle, our Cosmic Consciousness, considerations that should be equally acceptable to the thoughtful skeptic as to a devout member of the church. These subjects are as follows:

Forgiveness
Compassion
Love
Acceptance
Thirst for Truth
Sacrifice and
Devotion

Father, Forgive Them, for They Don't Know What They Are Doing

Luke 23:34
Subject: Forgiveness

The careful reader may wonder why Jesus prays to the Father to forgive his executioners rather than simply saying to them "You are forgiven." He has repeatedly indicated that by virtue of his divine nature, he had the power to forgive sins (Mt 9:2; Lk 5:24; Jn 5:27). He does not exercise that power because he is suffering as a human being subject to all the vulnerability of human nature. He receives no privilege; he suffers and prays as one of us might suffer and pray.

But Jesus's action goes further than forgiving a personal wrong. It is an example of praying for evildoers instead of condemning them. "Stop judging that you may not be judged" (Mt 7:1) has much wider implications than "forgive us as we forgive others" in the Lord's Prayer, and it is a more difficult challenge to follow. We are more likely to forgive our enemies whose ideas and emotions we share than to abstain from judgment against criminals and evildoers with whom we cannot identify. Whenever we hear about a crime involving violence, our first thought is usually about retribution, about a violent response, not that we should pity the offenders or pray for them but that they should be punished. Of course, we need punishments as deterrents as we need rewards for encouragement, but is it up to us to punish for the sake of retribution?

Speaking to some Christian advocates of law and order, especially on the subject of capital punishment, we are likely to hear, "The Bible says an eye for an eye and a tooth for a tooth." Jesus told us that that maxim is no longer valid, but it is as if these people have never read the New Testament.

The authors of the book *Beyond Repair? America's Death Penalty*, say that according to a Gallup poll conducted in June 1991, 50 percent of the responders who favored capital punishment said "a life for a life." Only 19 percent favored the death penalty as a "means to keep them from killing again." Another poll in 2000 coded 40 percent as saying "an eye for an eye," and an additional 13 percent were of the opinion that capital punishment "serves justice." The next numerous group of responders, 12 percent, did not want the state to spend money on keeping murderers alive. As for the deterrent value of capital punishment, only 13 percent gave it as a reason in 1991 and 8 percent in 2000. Most of the supporters—69 percent in 1991 and 71 percent in 1999—said they would favor capital punishment even if it were proven to have no deterrent value.[84]

Thus the sense of retributive justice is deeply ingrained in our thinking and our emotions. Researchers at the University of Zurich found that punishment of cheaters evokes activity in the dorsal striatum, the region of the brain experiencing pleasure or satisfaction.[85]

This desire for retribution, the view of it as a given ideal, is deducible from the earliest history of civilization when, in the absence of a legal penal system, the threat of personal vengeance was the only way to keep oneself and one's own safe. All adversaries knew that for any injury, they had to return an eye for an eye and a tooth for a tooth, or even more. The vengeful kin would survive and beget vengeful offspring as well as teaching them the ethics of revenge. Out of this attitude grew the concept of retributive justice, of deserved punishment. Society installed judges whose task it was to decide about guilt and innocence, a power also given to the supreme ruler of the country and projected into a supreme monarchical ruler of the world. Even polytheistic religions fostered a belief into vengeful deities, such as the Erinyes, who would punish any guilt, even one the perpetrator, such as Oedipus, may not have been aware of. It became a convenient way to explain disasters befalling seemingly innocent people. Job's comforters resort to that theory, and they despair because he is "righteous in his own eyes" (Jb 32:1).

This idea of retributive justice haunts us to this day; it is responsible for cycles of violence all over the world, and for hatred between groups of people caused by actual or imagined wrongs. It is also responsible for the satisfaction people feel when they see a culprit punished, even the "closure" some people experience when they see the murderer of a loved one put to death. But we no longer need this inherited mechanism of self-defense. We do not live in the jungle. When we are appalled by a crime and taking measures to prevent its recurrence, we ought to be able to experience some compassion as we become aware of the terrible darkness into which the soul of the criminal becomes immersed, the self-imposed punishment of being removed from God, or in nontheistic terms, from the community of life.

Does the criminal know what he is doing? We are profoundly caught up in the belief in free will and individual responsibility. We are unable to act without believing that our conscious act is "free."

Then again, we also know that our freedom is severely limited by factors over which we have no control: strong emotions, prejudices imprinted upon our minds since childhood, and so on. According to the *New England Journal of Medicine* more than half the inmates of our prisons have symptoms of a psychiatric disorder.[86] Where is the point of balance between freedom and the chain of cause and effect? Only an omniscient judge can decide. It is in this context that St. Paul writes, "Vengeance is mine, I shall repay, says the Lord" (Rom 12:19). And Jesus teaches us by his example to abstain from judgment and even to go further, doing an act of love by praying for the heartless, the cruel, the despicable ones.

We are far removed from such progress, yet most civilized countries—unfortunately only some of the United States—have taken one important step forward by abolishing capital punishment, pure revenge without any benefit to society.

There are two benefits of forgiveness extended to our enemies and offenders, a social and a metaphysical one. They should be considered separately to enhance the understanding of their importance.

The benefit of forgoing revenge in interpersonal relationships is obvious.

Retaliation practiced among groups of people is more malignant than retribution within a society, because it involves more lives, and may, if it ever results in a nuclear war, threaten the entire living community on earth. Most conflicts between groups arise because of competition for material goods, yet to be realized they have to almost always be clothed in ideals, such as freedom, destiny, equal rights, heroism, and so on. To this, more often than not, is added the conviction that the enemy is evil to the core. Such an assumption is needed to effectively combat an enemy, and it too arises from eons of competition of tribes and nations for material goods. The need for such competition has greatly diminished in modern times. What remains, however, is greed and the craving for power as well as suspicion and hatred among nations who are still susceptible to the belief that the enemy is intrinsically evil.

In his book *Frieden ist moeglich—Peace Is Possible,* the German author Franz Alt discusses the implications of Christian teachings controlling politics.[87] Earlier, Leo Tolstoy outlined the same principles in his treatise *The Kingdom of God Is Within You,*[88] a work that greatly influenced Mahatma Gandhi. "Turning the other cheek" (Mt 5:39) is a challenge that reaches further than mere rejection of retribution, but it certainly implies such rejection.

Of course, the Church teaches us that there is a God-given a priori principle of justice and required atonement. But even if we believe that, we must leave all judging to God since we are incapable of looking into the souls of men. Therefore, we should limit our actions to deterrent punishment, without which, so far at least, we cannot maintain an ordered society. But as long as the concept of retributive justice to which man is entitled and even obligated lingers in people's minds, a lasting peace between people and between nations will remain difficult to achieve.

The discussion of the practical benefits of Jesus's teachings is only incidental in the framework of this book. My contention is that these teachings point a way to the step-by-step achievement of Cosmic Consciousness. The belief that either individuals or groups are, in essence, evil, having freely chosen to be bad and thus deserving and even necessitating our dislike, *isolates us from each other, and it makes the realization of our mutual identity, a precondition to approaching*

Cosmic Consciousness, difficult. For that reason I question the validity of an ideal of deserved retribution and suspect that it is nothing but a deeply ingrained behavioral reflex developed through millennia of needing self-defense, a process I already mentioned. As much as I disagree with B. F. Skinner about moral principles being solely the result of reciprocal action,[60] I believe that the principle of guilt requiring punishment has developed in exactly that fashion and that, as I conjectured above, reward and punishment by God is another projection of qualities of a terrestrial ruler onto the divine image. We apply this idea of sinfulness requiring retribution to ourselves as well as to others, except that most of us feel that we are better than many other offenders, thus excluding them from the human community on the basis of value. But anytime we exclude someone from the fold, we isolate ourselves as well, even though we may belong to an overwhelming majority. For, no matter with whom we remain, the unity is broken. We have distanced ourselves from the totality of Being. It is thus that judgment is turned against him who judges.

In this context we may well consider another saying of Jesus: "You have heard that it was said to your ancestors: 'You shall not kill; and whoever kills shall be liable to judgment.' But I say to you, whoever is angry with his brother will be liable to judgment" (Mt 5:21–22). This again has two applications; from a point of view of daily life, anger is the source of violence and should be suppressed before it results in physical injury, but seen from a metaphysical standpoint, the injury to our innermost nature has already occurred. One does not have to go as far as killing to disrupt the community of beings. Hatred, scorn, and resentment will do the same. By realizing our enduring common essence, no matter into what erroneous paths it might be directed by its "psycho-physical stuff," we transcend all temporal events and attain eternal life. Any willful separation implied in considering one's own innermost self better than that of another, or hostile toward it, is self-destruction, perhaps symbolized by the consuming fire of Gehenna (Mt 5:22). For the higher we hold our individual worth, the more we isolate ourselves in our mortal shell. Just like someone who has offended us or society and whom we judge, we commit the fatal error of separation.

Amen, I Say to You, Today You Will Be with Me in Paradise

Luke 23:39–43
Subject: Compassion

There are two criminals or, as some translations say, revolutionaries crucified on each side of Jesus. One of them heaps abuse on Jesus, whereas the other one says, "Leave him alone. We are here because we deserve it, but he has done nothing wrong." And then, "Lord, remember me when you come into your kingdom." Jesus replies, "Today you will be with me in paradise."

In rebuking the other criminal, the man defending Jesus forgets his own agony and expresses compassion and disapproval of injustice. He thinks of another man besides himself. In that sense he is already with Jesus, not only because he expresses his support but also because he shares with Jesus, in a smaller way, the quality of giving of oneself.

All devout Christians want to be with Jesus in paradise. But Jesus's teaching commands us to be with him first here on earth, as was the man crucified at his side. That is the door to paradise, to eternal life, aside from any possible individual survival after death.

Through his suffering Jesus gives the man a chance to rehabilitate himself, to do a good deed in thought and in word. The suffering of others does the same for us.

According to Jesus, the people who are saved on "judgment day" are those "who saw him hungry and gave him food, thirsty and gave him drink, welcomed him as a stranger, clothed him when he was naked, cared for him when he was ill, visited him in prison" (Mt 25:35–36). If that is the criterion of salvation, how could we be "saved" without the suffering that we witness? As Jesus, by dying on the cross, makes it possible for the criminal to enter paradise, so do thousands of others give us that chance by suffering in our presence, within our reach. Made in the image of God we validate that image by stepping in, by doing his work wherever the need arises. The author Philip Yancey, who wrote extensively on the problem of pain, arrived at the same conclusion.[89]

One of my favorite passages in the New Testament is the answer Jesus gave when asked if the blind man he was about to cure was being punished for his own or his parents' sins. Jesus replied, "Neither he nor his parents sinned, it is so that the works of God might be made visible through him" (Jn 9:3). Jesus probably refers to the miraculous cure he will perform on this man, but many other acts of God are not necessarily miracles; they are our own works performed in accordance with our innermost divine nature, works of help and compassion, or even just comforting words like those of the crucified criminal.

All suffering unavoidably brings up the problem of theodicy, of reconciling the alleged all-powerful goodness of God with the existence of evil, cruelty, pain, and suffering. There can be only two answers to that dilemma: one that all pain is somehow compensated for and nullified, the other that evil is real and categorically necessary for the very existence of goodness. This latter view is compatible with the fact everyone may observe, namely, that whether there be people who "deserve" punishment or not, all evil—that is pain and suffering—are spread through the world arbitrarily like the spilled contents of Pandora's box.

I have already mentioned the experience of some individuals "that all things work together for the good of each and all"[71,72] associated with an almost unbearable sensation of perfection of the world. But such a revelation is not only inaccessible to most but has for us no practical importance. By the divine spark inherent in our innermost nature, we feel compelled to interfere wherever evil occurs.

If we believe in an afterlife, then according to Matthew's gospel quoted above, we are eventually rewarded for helping others, but even if we do not hold such beliefs, *our reward is here and now because we fulfill the desire of our innermost nature to live for and through others, a Self-realization that leads to Cosmic Consciousness, the understanding that we are part of a living cosmos and timeless by virtue of that unity.*

It is worthy of note that compassion does not add to our own misery, whatever it may be, but rather alleviates it for the believer and the atheist alike. The more concern I have for my neighbor's pain, the easier it is for me to cope with my own adversity. It is thus that my reward is here and now, but to those who believe in a hereafter, their faith offers additional hope.

Leo Tolstoy gave his book *The Kingdom of God Is Within You*[88] the subtitle *Christianity Not As a Mystic Religion But As a New Theory of Life.* This "new theory of life," life in this world, involves both unconditional forgiveness and limitless compassion, illustrated by the two first words of the crucified Savior. Here again we see the pairing of the practical and metaphysical aspects of Christianity.

This chapter concerns mainly our attitude toward the suffering of others, and the opportunities we receive by compassion in word and deed. I shall speak of dealing with our own misfortunes later.

One additional note for the careful reader: Jesus says, "Today you will be with me in paradise." But, according to the gospel of John, the risen Jesus tells Mary Magdalene, "I have not yet ascended to the Father" (Jn 20:17). Furthermore, according to the Acts of the Apostles, written by Luke, whose quote is under discussion here, Jesus appeared to various witnesses for forty days (Acts 1:3) until he bodily ascended into heaven (Acts 1:9). Did Luke forget what he wrote earlier or does *today* mean that after death, there is no time, that all eternity is today? Or does it mean that the crucified criminal is in paradise already, in the all-pervading kingdom of heaven, a concept to be discussed later?

Woman, Behold Your Son

John 19:26
Subject: Love

Whereas the First Word illustrates Jesus's teaching about forgiveness, and the Second about compassion, the Third Word brings up the question of love, not just the perfect universal love preached by Jesus when he proclaims the Word of God, but the everyday personal love and concern that he displays toward his mother and his disciple. He not only loved a disciple (Jn 13:23, 19:26, 21:7) but also "loved Martha and her sister and Lazarus" (Jn 11:5). Jesus wept over Lazarus's death and then raised him (Jn 11:35–44). Factual or not, this story conveys to us the life-giving power of love, for those whom we love live forever in our hearts. In that way love not only permits us to live beyond ourselves but also gives life to the deceased. And so, as a human being, Jesus bears within him the limited, personal love, the germ of the general love that he so strongly advocates.

After he challenges us to love our enemies (Mt 5:44), Jesus says, "For if you love those who love you, what recompense will you have? ... So, be perfect as your Father is perfect" (Mt 5:46, 48). On another occasion he says, "If you want to be perfect, go sell what you have and give it to the poor, and you will have treasure in heaven. Then come and follow me" (Mt 19:21).

The question arises what is meant by *perfection* here. It is a term that involves an unsurpassable ability to do or to be something. Everyone is eager to achieve perfection in whatever his or her chosen field of endeavor may be: sports, art, or any profession. A perfect being would be, for us, one completely conforming to all ideals to which we are beholden. But that which is our common supreme ideal is the fulfillment of our common innermost nature, the service to life, whose representative in a perfect form is God, the God within and around us. As representatives of individual existence we cannot be perfect, as our Father is, but nevertheless perfection must be our goal. This explanation unites both statements of Jesus cited above; perfection is perfect love. "Be perfect as your Father is perfect" means "try to love everyone and everything as your Father does," or, in other words, "conform to your innermost nature which is essentially divine and therefore strives for universal unity through unlimited love."

If we expand our image of God to that of a superior potentate, we must include specific perfections, such as justice and mercy. Luke's citation of Jesus to "be merciful just as your Father is merciful" (Lk 6:36) implies such an expansion. Matthew's version corresponds to John's "God is love" (1 Jn 4:8), not then necessarily a potentate.

In advocating perfect love, Jesus does not seem to put much stock in family relations as evidenced by Mark 3:31–35: "Your mother and your brothers and sisters are outside asking for you ... and looking around at those seated in the circle he said, 'Here are my mother and my brothers. For whoever does the will of God is my brother and sister and mother.'" There is an even stronger statement in Mark 10:29–30: "Amen, I say to you, there is no one who has given up house or brothers or sisters or mother or father or children or lands for my sake and for the sake of the gospel who will not receive a hundred times more now in the present age: houses and brothers and sisters and mothers and children and lands, with persecutions, and eternal life in the world to come." Matthew 19:29 and Luke 18:29–30 contain almost identical statements, although persecution is not mentioned. In the section dealing with the beatitudes, I discuss the fact that universal love readily leads to persecution because it must include individuals opposed to each other and thus will invariably injure someone's interests. Thus, persecution becomes part of the price we pay for the fulfillment of our innermost nature, for Cosmic Consciousness, for the realization of our identity with all that lives.

But universal love moving toward perfection, imitating divine love, is learned only in a progressive fashion. Being equally involved with individuals close to us and with the world is humanly impossible. And if I neglect my family for the sake of the poor and the unloved, I shall make my children feel unloved and abandoned. Children raised in such an unemotional way may develop a sense of duty but not necessarily the ability to love others. It seems that love must be experienced in order to be learned. Stephen G. Post says that "no child who does not experience being loved will be able to pass it on to others."[90] A caricature of a mother neglecting her children's emotional needs while being involved in works of charity has been drawn by Charles Dickens in the character of Mrs. Jellyby in *Bleak House*.

We can derive from the accounts in the Gospels that Jesus was raised by concerned parents; they fled to Egypt to save him (Mt 2:13–15), and they worried about him when he stayed behind in Jerusalem when he decided to remain "in his Father's house" (Lk 2:41–49). Jesus repeatedly illustrates the love of God by the example of the love that a father extends to his children (e.g., Mt 7:9–10 or Lk

11:11–12), and his own personal love I mentioned in the beginning of this chapter. Therefore even Jesus's own words imply that personal love beginning at home is not something essentially opposed to universal love but rather is the beginning thereof. It may, of course, be truncated, stopped at the level of close relatives, as manifested by nepotism, or a little further, involving the nation or a group, denying affection or even harboring hatred toward other nations or groups.

I am told that when the Nazi criminal Adolf Eichmann was kidnapped by Israeli agents, he begged them not to hurt his children. The agents replied that they were not after his children, but they wondered if he ever worried about the Jewish children he had sent to their deaths. "Well, they were Jews" was Eichmann's reply. I cannot find any documentation of that story, but it illustrates the common phenomenon of truncated love, and I am sure that if it did not happen, the attitude displayed here is not difficult to find elsewhere.

Instead of being cut off so near its roots, our love should be like a circle of waves caused by a stone dropped on the calm surface of a lake. The circle should expand weakened but never completely stopped to the most distant shore. Thomas Aquinas has recognized this phenomenon as "ordering of love" already mentioned,[91] and the Stoics believed that through ever-widening circles of concern we become "citizens of the cosmos."[92]

How do we achieve such ordered expansion? In my introductory remarks, under the heading of "Love," I observed that expanded love requires identification with others, not a possessive desire involving only the id or the ego for its exclusive benefit. Such identification is strongest in our immediate environment. It may be a close relationship with a spouse or a friend, or a sharing of a common heritage of genes and culture, such as belonging to a family or a country, or being involved in a common purpose as a member of an organization toward which one feels loyalty and devotion. A thoughtful person will furthermore find identity with his or her environment and love and preserve nature and finally realize an identity with the entire universe. For everyone shares one's innermost nature, the will to live, with all that exists. We all belong together because we all constitute life, because we all carry the spark of divinity within us, because in our innermost essence we are made in our Creator's image. In loving the plenum of existence, the religious person loves God. The agnostic or the atheist, if he or she follows the impulse of his or her innermost nature, cannot help but love the essence of life or find his or her existence without purpose.

The progressive realization of identity must unite us even with the most cruel and despicable human being, within whom, however hidden, abused, and distorted, we should recognize our own essence. But here again, such realization is unlikely to occur unless love, trust, and tolerance have been learned in the circle of a family.

This brings up the problem of sexual love, without which neither a loving family nor procreation and with it perfection of the human race would be possible. I have observed already that most of our basic drives, such as hunger and thirst and even breathing, involve consumption of resources, and that the very existence of an individual necessitates some degree of competition with other beings. The sexual drive, on the other hand, involves unity and surrender of individuality. The fact that it may be abused as a tool of possession, control, and even violence does not contradict that insight. It is apparently also possible for some people to sublimate the sexual drive in other accomplishments. "Some have renounced marriage for the sake of the kingdom of heaven" (Mt 19:12). This statement refers to "some" who prefer a monastic life. If that is in their nature, they should follow it. But this is hardly a reason to denigrate sexuality and sanctify celibacy as an ideal for everyone. The only reason to do so lies in viewing this world as somehow evil and opposed to God, a belief espoused by Manichaeism and Gnosticism.[93] In that case any pleasurable activity and anything that serves life on this earth would be either wicked or at least not worthwhile, and Yahweh, who saw that what he created was good (Gn1:31) and who told man and woman to be fertile and multiply (Gn 1:28), is not the principle of our innermost nature. In that case, there is no point in improving life on this earth except as a trial preceding deliverance from this "valley of tears." But Jesus's teaching is directed toward improving the lot of others by validating our identity with them and with the world as a whole. This world contains many challenges to be conquered (Jn 16:33), but it is a world created by God, a work to be celebrated. If it is so, then Jesus's message cannot contain a condemnation of sexuality, nor is there one to be found in the Gospels.

Matthew Fox in his book *The Coming of the Cosmic Christ* devotes a chapter to the renaissance of sexual mysticism, emphasizing the creative, life-giving function of sexuality and its relation to creation-centered Christianity.[94]

The process of uniting physically is the elementary expression of love reaching down to the simplest chemical reactions and to the ringlike copulation of the bisexual earthworms. It continues to develop in the often involved and complex mating rituals of the animal kingdom and finds its apotheosis in the loving encounter of humans.

In addition to Gnostic influence, the condemnation of sex by the Christian churches arises from the idea that a strong drive toward another person derails our desire for a union with God, whereas I would rather view such a drive as a step toward reestablishment of that union. For even though we strive for universal love, sexual love limited to one person implies dedication and commitment that, again, is likely to be the germ of universal love rather than its opposite. Thus, we must hope that pure sexual release, urgently needed by most young people, does not remain in that truncated stage, but eventually leads to love, commitment, and fidelity. From here the circles on the surface of the waters may expand to the ends of the world.

It is not unusual to hear that the sin of Adam and Eve consisted in sexual intercourse based on the close resemblance of the snake to a phallus and the sexual aspect of the nakedness Adam and Eve become aware of after committing their sin. But God supplied them with sexual organs and told them to multiply, which speaks against the sinfulness of sexual intercourse. Furthermore, the snake, even allowing for its phallic resemblance, has multiple other symbolic meanings,[95] including an association with heathen rites that would be considered deadly for a devotee of Yahweh.[96] The serpent may also represent death by its ability to administer a fatal sting.[97] Such a fatality has occurred at the point of creation of individual life that for its very existence depends on mortality. Even before my final death, I die and am born anew as a different being in every moment of time. The difference between all other creatures and man is the latter's awareness of his mortality, the *knowledge* of the essential good and evil, of the continuous presence of death. Adam and Eve are upset by their nakedness not because it reveals their sexuality but because it represents being exposed to the danger of the world with limited means of defense, being on one's own, a significance recognized by Pope John Paul II.[98]

Sexual abstinence is for some people a form of dedication to God, as I have discussed, but in its essence is not a perfection of such a dedication. Sexual union is a service to life, to unity, to God. It is wrong to elevate sexual abstinence to an ideal for everyone, and the emphasis placed on such abstinence by the Christian churches is mistaken. In his afterword to the Kreutzer Sonata[99] Leo Tolstoy, apparently feeling guilty about the sexual excesses of his youth, echoes the sentiments of St. Augustine and advocates sexual abstinence. He counters the objection that it would lead to an elimination of the human race by the obvious fact that there is absolutely no danger of all humanity following his advice. But a recommendation that is good only if it is rarely followed is hardly to be taken seriously.

It is interesting to note that St. John Climacus in his book *Scala (Klimax) Paradisi* ("The Ladder to Paradise") is cited by the Russian philosopher Nikolai Berdyaev as saying, "One who tends toward sensuality is compassionate and merciful, but those tending toward purity are not so."[100] This foremost authority on asceticism recognized the germ of love inherent in sexuality.

The Hindu concept of different stages of life where a man proceeds from being a student to being a "householder" and then to attaining ascesis and wisdom in later life recognizes the progression from sexuality toward spirituality without their mutual exclusion.[101] Such a progression is meaningless without the element of love, without the ultimate realization of our innermost nature, common to all.

The ultimate achievement of perfection, "as our Father is perfect," *would involve universal identification without loss of intensity with* *increasing distance from us, absolute forgiveness, and endless compassion.* This is what we must desire, unattainable as it may be for us. Jesus, in dying for the entire humanity out of limitless love, is "made perfect through suffering" (Heb 2:10). But as a dying fully human being, he reverts to the beginnings of that love in which we all partake, the individual love, in his case that of his mother and his disciple. Therein lies the importance of this Third Word from the cross, whether it be historically accurate or only "reflecting the writer's special interests," meaning those of "the disciple whom Jesus loved."[102]

In presenting Christianity as a way toward Cosmic Consciousness, I have used a number of concepts found in Hinduism. Most of these concepts can be easily related to the development of progressive love. But what is unique about Christianity is love proving itself in a painful self-sacrifice.

My God, My God, Why Have You Forsaken Me?

Mark 15:34
Subject: Acceptance

The next two utterances of Jesus leave no doubt that his suffering was human, emotional in the feeling of abandonment and physical in the terrible sensation of thirst. In the despair of abandonment, Jesus joins the countless people who must have experienced and, no doubt, will experience hopelessness as long as humans live: the little girl raped and buried alive, a drowning person who has accidentally fallen overboard, the defenseless victim of genocide being marched to his or her death.

Once again we are faced with the problem of evil that exists despite the goodness of God, the never resolved subject of theodicy. We have already decided that rather than questioning the reasons for evil and the pain caused by people and circumstances, we must counter this evil with compassion and active help. But that only constitutes the meaning of another person's suffering for the observer, for the compassionate helper who fulfills his divine nature by stepping in. But if no help is forthcoming and the only imaginable end of suffering is death, the sufferer may well despair. Can any justification be found for such a situation, any meaning, anything positive?

There is a story in the gospel of Luke (Lk 16:19–31), quoted and read quite frequently, that I find disturbing.[103] A man who enjoys riches and a sumptuous life goes to eternal torment in hell, whereas a man by the name of Lazarus who subsisted on the rich man's garbage and was covered with sores licked by dogs is carried after his death to the bosom of Abraham. What disturbs me is that the rich man's only fault mentioned here, even though he may well have had many, is his comfortable life, and Lazarus' only merit mentioned is his misery. Should we then be afraid of being happy? Should we seek misery? And why help others if they will be rewarded in proportion to their suffering, nay, even in excess thereof, for the heavenly bliss is eternal and the earthly misery can last but a lifetime. It is also easier to accept eternal bliss as a reward for temporary suffering than eternal damnation for a relatively brief lifetime of happiness.

Of course, as Jesus points out (Mt 19:24), the rich may not care for spiritual goods and thus be eternally separated from God, and Abraham refers the rich man to Moses and the prophets with their exhortations to share wealth as, for example, in Isaiah 58:7. Thus, the rich man may be guilty of ignoring the misery of others and be punished for that transgression rather than just for being rich. Still, Lazarus' main virtue appears to be his suffering. Such a reward in the hereafter is a great comfort for one who remains firm in his or her belief in the justice of God while facing a situation without hope, without meaning for his or her life on earth, a life that is about to end.

I must admit that deep within, I have a faith in divine Providence and some superior wisdom guiding my life. Still, I do not understand how anyone can live without harboring some intellectual doubt about such supernatural direction. And some individuals are probably sincere in denying it altogether. What comfort can I have if, being such a person, I am faced with hopeless suffering and a painful death? Can these things have any positive meaning for me?

Viktor Frankl founded a school of psychotherapy he called logotherapy, based on man's searching for meaning and finding it even in hopeless situations. As Frankl points out, it is pathological and masochistic to seek suffering, but once it is unavoidable, it is up to the person to find meaning in it, if only by turning it into an achievement.[104] It is easy, of course, to find meaning in suffering that one has survived, and even death can have a positive significance; it may be a sacrifice for a cause, a country, one's own family, or it may represent an atonement or a test of strength. In dying, Jesus utters seven phrases, all of which lend meaning to his death. But my question is now whether suffering per se can be meaningful apart from any redeeming detail.

To illuminate this problem I will again take recourse to the love of a person. It has nothing to do with positive qualities of the beloved; it is the unconditional dedication to the object of love, a dedication of which women are probably more often capable than men. It is especially apparent in a mother's love. Love of life has the same quality. People cling to life even under the most adverse circumstances and accept adversity as part of it. Life is a mixture of happiness and misery, none of these two opposites having any meaning without the other. Therefore, in loving life, I must accept its dark side as I accept the bad qualities of a person I love. I accept adversity not because I deserve it but because it is part of the precious gift of life. In the book of Job we found a quote expressing that very insight: "We accept good things from God; and should we not accept evil?" (Jb 2:10). Substitute *life* for *God* and the statement will become true even to an atheist.

We can validate our essential unity with God, the Principle of Life, by fully embracing the manifestation of that principle, by embracing the cosmos as it has to be. Fully accepting suffering as part of life is a giant step toward Cosmic Consciousness, yet we must keep in mind that only unavoidable suffering is to be accepted. Seeking pain deliberately for the sole purpose of suffering pain is masochism, which does not serve life.

Thus, whereas our attitude toward the suffering of others must be compassion and help whenever possible, that toward our own unavoidable misfortunes must be acceptance. The basis for the first is our identity with others. The basis for both is our identity with the Principle of Life whose representatives we are, a principle that requires adversity for its manifestation. It is a commonly heard adage that "life is not fair," and I have already remarked that evil is spread arbitrarily throughout the world. But this "unfairness" is not an unfortunate by-product of life, but rooted in life's very essence.

Growing up in Nazi Germany, I frequently saw the prominently displayed slogan *"Leben heisst kämpfen. Sag Ja zum Leben!"* (To live is to fight. Say Yes to life!) This was an abused quotation of Seneca, who, in his *Letters* says, *"Vivere militare est,"*[105] abused because the Nazis used it to justify their aggressive behavior, including their war machine. But Seneca's thought is not that of justifying aggression; he rather sees life as going "uphill and downhill over toilsome crags and heights." Seneca, of course, means that acceptance of adversity is necessary if we want to live, whereas we add here that that very fact, once properly understood, is a condition for imparting us into cosmic life, fulfilling our desire to be part of life in general, in addition to participating in "ever growing circles of concern," the Stoic view mentioned earlier.[92] According to Matthew Fox, "without naming our pain and lamenting our situation, no prophets are shaped or born. No true creativity can occur.[106]

Acceptance of adversity qua part of life causes our appreciation of works of art representing such adversity. The art works of Goya and Kaethe Kollwitz, as well as novels by Thomas Hardy and many others, are enjoyed for precisely that reason. Of course, enjoying such works is limited to contemplating suffering of others, and sometimes our own, already overcome. But will I be able to apply my philosophy to myself facing pain and death in a hopeless situation? "… 'tis a consummation devoutly to be wished."[107]

5

I Thirst

John 19:28
Subject: Thirst for Truth

The complete quote is as follows: "After this, aware that everything was now finished, in order that the scripture might be fulfilled, Jesus said: I thirst. There was a vessel filled with common wine. So they put a sponge soaked in wine on a sprig of hyssop and put it to his mouth." The New Jerusalem Bible speaks of "sour wine," whereas other translations, including the German one by Martin Luther, say "vinegar." In Matthew 27:48 and in Mark 15:36 it is a reed that is used to lift the sponge to Jesus's mouth. The scriptures being fulfilled by the Fourth and this, the Fifth, Words are two quotations from Psalms: one from Psalm 22 (verses 2 and 16) starting with "My God, my God, why have you abandoned me" and later, "As dry as a potsherd is my throat; my tongue sticks to my palate; you lay me in the dust of death"; and one from Psalm 69:22, which says, "Instead they put gall in my mouth; for my thirst they gave me vinegar."[108]

The entire scene is that of a dying victim of crucifixion, severely dehydrated, and an act of mockery, or perhaps a left-handed attempt to help, by a bystander. No other meaning may have been intended by the Gospel writers. The thirst of a person dying from exposure and dehydration on a cross was terrible. But the symbolism of water is so important in all of the New Testament that Jesus's asking for it and receiving a poor substitute becomes pregnant with additional meaning and demands a recapitulation and, ideally, an explanation of the things Christ received from his followers instead of those he asked for.

Water is essential for life. It necessarily pervades all living beings and thus symbolizes the universal life-giving force. It also denotes cleansing, symbolically applied to our spirit.[109] Both meanings are contained in the rite of baptism.

Jesus compares the truth to which he testifies (Jn 18:37) to "a spring of water welling up to eternal life" (Jn 4:14). We thirst for that truth because "it will set us free" (Jn 8:32). Free from what? It will set us free from the fear of death, and will set us free to follow the drive of our innermost nature. The encounter with the Samaritan woman described in the fourth chapter of the gospel of John with its reference to water that once tasted eliminates thirst forever has been described as "a paradigm of our engagement with truth."[110] No one will disagree that this truth has been abused and distorted to the point of being unrecognizable in the behavior of avowed Christians.

As I have attempted to show in the preceding and the following text, the essence of Jesus's teaching is the realization of universal unity through love. The violence that has often dominated the practice of the Christian faith is diametrically opposed to that original intent. Can we find reasons for such a distortion?

Clearly, Jesus anticipated the misuse of his legacy when he said, "Do not think that I have come to bring peace upon the earth. I have come not to bring peace but the sword" (Mt 10:34). The same is expressed almost verbatim in the gospel of Luke (Lk 12:51).

The violence perpetrated in the name of Christianity is at least as obvious as any good done in the name of Christ. The Crusades with the sacking of Constantinople in 1204, the Thirty-Year War between Catholics and Protestants from 1618 to 1648 that devastated central Europe, the machinations and cruelty of the Inquisition, and the hanging of "witches" in Salem are all well-known historical facts. The Nazi Holocaust was not a religious persecution, but it would not have been possible without the anti-Semitism that had been fostered for centuries by church authorities. The pogroms in Tsarist Russia were definitely motivated by "Christian" zeal. Between September 16 and 18, 1982, Christian Lebanese Phalangists murdered at least 700, possibly as many as 3,500 (depending on the source) Palestinian refugees in the Sabra and Shatilla camps in Lebanon.[111] We do not know whether any of these men were churchgoing Christians, but be that as it may, it was an attack on Moslems by individuals identifying themselves as followers of Christ. It is also quite likely that, churchgoing or not, many if not most of these murderers were "good people" in the framework of their local communities and their families. We do not have to dig far into our history to find "men of God," leaders of the church, again "good people," lending their support to mayhem, such as the extermination of Native Americans. In 1631, the Puritan leader Cotton Mather rejoiced that "God ended the controversy by sending the smallpox among the Indians ... who were before that time exceedingly numerous."[112] The Christian colonizers definitely believed God to be on their side. Thus the Plymouth governor William Bradford said, "It was a fearful sight to see them thus frying in the fire and the streams of blood quenching the same, and horrible was the stink and scent thereof; but the victory seemed a sweet sacrifice, and they gave the praise thereof to God who had wrought so wonderfully for them, thus to enclose their enemies in their hands and give them so speedy a victory over so proud and insulting an enemy."[113] How are all these acts and words by religious Christians possible? Or perhaps we should ask how all this mayhem can be reconciled with the perpetrators' religious beliefs, for wars and atrocities would have certainly occurred without the benefit of Christianity.

It seems that in all these cases of violence, the Christian religion has become a means of identification, such as membership in a nation whose views and goals may change, rather than a set of teachings to be followed. The roots of such identification with the person of Jesus apart from his message go back to the earliest days of Christianity.

When Jesus is asked by an official (Lk 18:18–23) what he should do to inherit eternal life, his answer is to follow the Ten Commandments and, in addition, "to be perfect," give his possessions to the poor. In the gospel of Mark, Jesus tells one of the scribes that the greatest commandments are to love God and to love one's neighbor as oneself (Mk 12:30–31). All these statements imply active charity, mercy, and love. But when the jailor of Paul and Silas (Acts 16:30–31), about to be converted, asks, "What shall I do to be saved?" the answer is "Believe in the Lord Jesus, and you and your household will be saved." And then there is the famous passage in the letter of Paul to the Romans, "For we consider that a person is justified by faith apart from the works of the law" (Rom 3:28). Paul is trying to say that the Gentiles do not have to adhere to the innumerable laws imposed upon the Jews to be saved, and that works without faith cannot lead to salvation. He does not deny the need to love one's neighbor, who may even be one's enemy. Martin Luther, who felt that no matter how he lived he could not be justified before God because of his inherent sinfulness and clung to the grace promised by faith, did not suggest ignoring Jesus's moral challenges either. But how easily can Silas' and Paul's statements lead us to believe that works are of a secondary importance, how easy is it in fact to justify even violence in the defense of the saving faith! The letter of James anticipates the dangers of pure faith in the person of Jesus without due regard for his teachings. The introduction to that letter in the 1970 edition of the New American Bible quotes Luther as saying that emphasis on good works found therein does not agree with St. Paul's doctrine of justification by faith. My foregoing comments illustrate the dangers of that doctrine.

The Didache, a text stemming from the first or, at the latest, the mid-second century AD.[114] and containing instructions for early Christian communities, begins with the words "There are two ways; one of life and one of death. And there is a great difference between the two ways. On the one hand the way of life is this: first you will love the God who made you, second: you will love your neighbor as yourself."[115] It continues by enlarging on these principles. But the earliest creed of the Christian church leadership, the Apostles' Creed—not contained in the Didache—composed in the West in the late second century[116] and subsequently amended and enlarged by several church councils, does not mention those essential teachings at all. Instead it speaks of the virgin birth, the descent into hell, the bodily ascension into heaven, the second coming, and so on. This creed is recited by churchgoing Christians every Sunday, whereas the resolve to love God and one's neighbor, the essential teaching of Jesus, does not constitute an obligatory part of the service. But if the belief in a set of supernatural events is the sine qua non of salvation, then any doubt of the truth of these events must be eradicated and anyone who might deceive people in believing otherwise must be eliminated, for what is death, even a gruesome one such as being burned at the stake, compared with eternal damnation for "heresy," a concept nowhere mentioned by Jesus?

Viewing Jesus not as a teacher but as a power to be worshipped, a decisive split of person and word, was accomplished by the Emperor Constantine, who had the vision of a cross in the sky before the battle of the Milvian Bridge in AD 312 and decided that he won with the aid of Jesus.[117] At that ancient juncture the power of Christ was split away in the human mind from the truth of Christ. Christianity gained the status of an official religion because of the belief that Jesus took sides in a secular battle, the very epitome of hostility, the very opposite of love leading to a realization of unity craved by our innermost nature as the source of life. It is that craving for life that Jesus points to when he tells his disciple to put away the sword (Mt 26:52), not just a practical piece of advice. "All who take the sword will perish by the sword" not only physically but also spiritually. This does not refer to those who are obligated to bear arms but to those who believe in violence as a chosen way of life; the sword here may be taken as symbol of an attitude.

Unfortunately, the use of the sword is sanctioned by the historical accounts of the Old Testament, and the revolting statements of the early Christian settlers of America mentioned above are in keeping with their belief that they, as Christians, were the legitimate heirs of the chosen people of Israel. Jesus left behind all the mayhem reported by the Bible and allegedly representing the actions of God, and introduced a new kind of chosen people, those for whom the love of others is supreme law. It is high time that we follow Jesus in that regard. We do not even have to try to decide whether any slaughter of Israel's enemies was the will of God; as Christians we must assume that the teachings of Jesus supersede anything that the Old Testament may tell us.

Constantine probably did not doubt his right to wage war for the sake of the expansion of his power. This was not the view of church authorities. St. Augustine of Hippo (AD 354–AD 430), one of the most influential doctors of the church, did not believe in any war fought for a cause that was not just, and he obviously was disturbed by the horrors of war. He writes, "The real evils in war are love of violence, revengeful cruelty, fierce and implacable enmity, wild resistance, and the lust of power and such like."[118] Behind this statement is the insight that war involves the destruction of mutual love and unity, the death of the soul by the sword. The only "just war," then, is one corresponding to justifiable defensive violence. Punitive action in war must also be of a defensive nature, "for to take delight in the suffering of those upon whom even just vengeance is visited is itself an injustice, and thus to do so runs counter to the aims for which just wars are fought."[119] And yet, according to Augustine, a war can also be just if it is started upon the decree of God conveyed through a divinely ordained oracle, such as Moses or Joshua.[120] Because anyone can claim to be such a divinely ordained oracle, not only the bloodshed described in the Old Testament, the one Augustine attempts to justify, but also subsequent acts of violence, such as that aimed at the extermination of Native Americans, can be explained away. All that is required is the conviction that God is on your side, and in the case of some religious Christians, that you are fighting in the name of the person of Jesus, regardless of what he may have taught.

A recent example of a separation of Jesus from his message can be found in a *Los Angeles Times* news story. An American sniper deployed in Iraq had placed a tattoo of a Crusader cross on his arm, saying, "I wanted everyone to know that I was a Christian … I hated the damn savages I was fighting."[121] This man, who was shot to death by someone he was trying to help, was a hero, a good man, and a religious man who had done his duty in the armed forces and was trying to help others. We cannot object to his killing the enemy, because sometimes this is unavoidable. But it has nothing to do with

Christianity, and any attempt to integrate it into one's definition of a Christian is wrong and leads to an abuse of that concept.

Part of the reason Jesus's person is worshipped instead of his teaching is the fact that the latter is too difficult to be followed literally. This has been commented upon by Leo Tolstoy.[122] He says correctly that whereas Judaism and Islam give specific instructions for handling difficult situations, the New Testament contains many hyperbolic statements that point the way toward perfection but are impossible to follow to a full extent. It is not always possible to "turn the other cheek" or to forgo resisting evil. A criminal must be forcefully restrained, and common sense tells us that we have the right to defend ourselves against any serious injury by others. Therefore we "throw the baby out with the bathwater" and ignore Jesus's words altogether, forgetting that all his statements are ultimately challenges to move toward the fulfillment of our innermost nature to the best of our ability. Therefore, instead of distilling the principles of love and unity out of the often confusing texts of the Gospels and taking them to be the most important ones, we choose the easier ones prescribed by the Church, such as tithing, fasting, attending mass, and so on.

In adhering to prescriptions of the Church as well as to the moral rules of society, we encounter another deviation from the ultimate goal set for us by Jesus, namely to transcend our individual limits by loving and caring for others. Instead, we, all good people, observe rules that will earn us tit-for-tat rewards, a thoroughly selfish enterprise, another way of handing Jesus vinegar instead of water.

Meister Eckhart addresses this issue in a sermon about Jesus driving the traders out of the temple, a dwelling place of God, which he equates to the human being whose inner essence is made in the likeness of God:

> I shall now preach exclusively about good people. Nevertheless, I shall make clear at this time who the traders were, and still are, who thus bought and sold and still do it, whom our Lord beat and drove out of the Temple ... See, all those are traders who avoid gross sins and do good deeds to the honor of God, such as fasting, waking, praying, and whatever else there is of that sort, all kinds of good works, yet they do them only with the purpose that God may give them something or do something for them that they might like; all these are traders.[123]

In this context it would also be appropriate to cite the Sufi saint Rabi'a: "I am going to burn paradise and douse hellfire, so that both veils may be lifted from those on the quest and they become sincere of purpose. God's servants will learn to see him without hope for reward or fear of punishment. As it is now, if you took away hope for reward or fear of punishment no one would worship or obey."[124] And Berdyaev writes, "The idea of personal salvation is transcendental egotism, the projection of egotism unto eternal life. The relation to God becomes profit seeking and pure spirituality is rendered impossible."[125] The same thought is expressed by Schleiermacher and quoted in my introduction to this essay.

Among the observances recommended by the Church as a way toward salvation, chastity—meaning a complete abstention from sexual activity—occupies a prominent place. In some cases, a loving person may remain chaste so that all egotistic desire for physical satisfaction may be removed from his or her relations with others. But it also may and often does become an egotistic form of self-chastisement, another way of bargaining for points of merit before God.

It must finally be said that asking God for forgiveness involves a selfish desire to escape punishment. This concept must therefore be reevaluated as an important factor in approaching Cosmic Consciousness. It should denote renewal, transcending the burden of the past rather than avoiding deserved retribution. I discuss that aspect of transgressions in the sections on mourning and mercy.

The symbolism of sour wine offered to Jesus instead of water may evoke images of misdeeds of the Church: the actions of a pope such as Alexander VI, the selling of indulgences by Pope Julian, and, of course, the incidents of sexual abuse by priests and other clergymen that have recently come to light. All these people knew that they were not in tune with their religion. They either did not care or were troubled by guilt. Such individuals do not foster a following.

It is the "good people" who distort Jesus's message, think themselves to be in the right, and even look down on others. They are referred to in the gospel of Luke where a Pharisee says, "O God, I thank you that I am not like the rest of humanity—greedy, dishonest, adulterous—or even like this tax collector. I fast twice a week and I pay tithes on my whole income" (Lk 18:9–14). He is certainly a good man, but he "did not go home justified," because he used his goodness to exalt himself and to be rewarded. He is also the one likely to be admired and imitated while he hands sour wine to the crucified Savior. The tax collector, on the other hand, who is a "bad man," goes home justified because he humbles himself and in doing so abandons an egocentric attitude. Placing oneself above the crowd implies separation, as does passing judgment over others. In humbling oneself, one joins the throng of life.

There are three ways in which good people hand Jesus vinegar instead of water:

One is worshipping his person independently from the essential principles of self-transcendence he proclaimed, which may lead to deadly stagnation in ritual and often to violence.

Another is interpreting Jesus's teachings as a set of laws that God might enforce by reward or punishment rather than as a guide to self-fulfillment.

Finally, it is rewarding oneself for virtuousness by considering oneself better than others. It must be said that a sense of inferiority in excess of humbleness has the same effect. We must remain aware of our value as agents of life and representatives of God through our innermost Self. We must submit to others out of love, not out of a sense of worthlessness.

It is, of course, not possible to order someone to become aware of their innermost nature and to move toward Self-realization through love, whereas it is possible to demand that people follow certain rules of behavior mindful of others and to enforce these rules by rewards and punishments. And yet, if we assume that our innermost nature is forever seeking Self-realization, should we not also assume that following such rules will eventually resonate in our hearts and minds and open them to the true essence of our being and the immortality it implies?

It Is Finished

John 19:30
Subject: Sacrifice

The Greek word that John uses is *tetelestai,* which in the New Jerusalem Bible is translated "it is fulfilled." Martin Luther's translation says the same: *"Es ist vollbracht,"* and the Russian, Spanish, and French translations of the New Testament in my library use words with a similar meaning. Jesus has done what he set out to do. "My food is to do the will of the one who sent me and to finish his work" (Jn 4:34). But what was that work, apparently referring to Jesus's entire ministry and to his ultimate sacrifice? If we perceive in his teachings and in his self-sacrifice a challenge to step out of our selfish confines and realize our unity with the One Creative Principle—in other words progress toward Cosmic Consciousness—at least conceptually, Jesus's teachings and deeds fall into place.

It is clear from Jesus's words at the Last Supper that he considered himself a sacrificial victim (Mt 26:28; Mk 14:24; Lk 22:19), as was the lamb whose blood, sprinkled on the door of a house, permitted death to pass over that habitation and made it possible for the family living there to escape death and, soon thereafter, captivity (Ex 12:3–13). The Evangelist goes as far as interpreting the lack of need to break Jesus's legs because he is already dead (Jn 19:33–36) as the fulfillment of a biblical prescription regarding the Passover Lamb (Ex 12:46). The symbolism found in the Exodus story by many Jewish interpreters is that of escape from whatever restrains us from serving our true self and in doing so, serving God.[126]

The slaughtering of the lamb or of a goat at full moon in the first month of spring was an ancient custom that became sacrificial on the night of the Passover and as such, according to Rabbi Nathan Laufer, represents a "closeness offering." That is, according to Laufer, the proper translation of the Hebrew word for sacrifice—*korban.*[127] But getting closer to God means, according to all that I have said so far, sacrificing some of your interests, of some part of your life, either directly to God or to some fellow being, thus permitting you to live outside your mortal limits. This life-giving aspect of sacrifice is clearly contained in the Exodus story, for death passes over those who display the blood of the lamb, and it becomes central in the Christian religion, leading to an "exodus" from sin and death. Sin is the opposite of sacrifice; sins are selfish acts consisting of hurting others and hurting oneself by decreasing one's devotion to the universal Principle of Life. Therefore, according to St. Paul, "the wages of sin is death, but the gift of God is eternal life in Christ Jesus our Lord" (Rom 6:23). Sacrifice then is a giving, a payment, not representing a fine or a punishment but rather an entrance fee we pay for a life beyond ourselves, *not payment for sin but an overcoming of sin and of death, both being the fate of limited individual life that is always somehow opposed to the life of others.* That is the symbolism we can derive from the blood of the lamb, as well as from the blood of the animals sacrificed by the high priest on the Day of Atonement.

But Jesus, by his example, teaches us that such vicarious sacrifice is inadequate, that we must be able to give of our own substance to realize our identity with the all-pervading Principle of Life, and he sacrifices himself as an example *for* us. Through sacrifice we give up our precious individuality and are stripped down to our innermost nature, which is life and which we share with others and with God, life's foremost principle. The former communion is represented symbolically by the horizontal beam of the cross, the latter by the vertical beam.[128] The life-giving communion is the reward of sacrifice, aside from any possible reward in the afterlife, which is thought to be uncertain albeit not denied here. This view is expressed by the bold statement in the apocryphal gospel of Philip: "Those who say that the Lord first died and then was resurrected are wrong; for he was first resurrected and then he died. If someone has not been resurrected they can only die. If they have already been resurrected, they are alive as God is alive."[129] Later it says, "Those who say that we are first die and then are resurrected are wrong. Whoever is not resurrected before death knows nothing and will die."[130] Feuerbach expressed the same thought when he said, "Death can be conquered only before death."[131] Such statements do not disprove the canonical accounts of resurrection, but they secure for them a significance beyond that of a miraculous event based on the divinity of Jesus. They tell us that having known death after tasting the fruit of the Tree of Knowledge of Good and Evil, we can enjoy the fruit of the Tree of Life by stepping out of our individual mortal confines by sacrifice. Death itself is a sacrifice every living being brings to life, because death defines life. Still, until our time comes, our will to live dictates that we postpone that sacrifice.

Obviously, premature sacrificial death requires an object. Killing myself only to prove my devotion to others would be absurd.

Therefore Jesus's sacrifice, aside from showing us a way of giving oneself to others, must have a definite purpose.

A traditional view of the Church has been that proposed by St. Anselm, namely that the sin of Adam, the original sin, representing an infinite offense, could be paid for, atoned, only by infinite love and sacrifice, those by the incarnate God himself.[132]

The concept of an original sin to be paid for is not part of the Jewish religion. It is not that which is atoned for during the high holidays but simply the people's daily, unavoidable, constantly committed sins. The Jewish religion does not believe in the reality of an inherited sin; every human being is born sinless.[133] Pelagius, in the fifth century, held the same view declared a heresy by Pope Zosimus in 418.[134] Matthew Fox in his book *Original Blessing* places a particular emphasis on the lack of a concept of the basic, hereditary depravity of man before that concept became dogmatic in the Christian church. He contrasts fall/redemption spirituality with what he calls "creation centered" spirituality, which may be seen as an approach to salvation through Cosmic Consciousness, through joining what I described using Whitehead's words as the "creative advance into novelty." Yet Fox stresses the existence of a "basic sin" of separateness tied to individual existence that treats others as objects, precisely what I believe is symbolized by the "fall of man," a fall only as a symbolic, not a historical, occurrence.[135] Fox also refers to numerous mystics who have held the same view. Yet we have to remember that Being per se can be manifested only as individual being, thus rendering the existence of the "basic sin of the necessary fault" unavoidable. All our avoidable transgressions of which we are guilty are derived from the original, unavoidable fault of self-centered existence.

Jesus himself is nowhere quoted as saying that he is atoning for the sin of Adam. His words according to Matthew 26:28 are "this is my blood of the covenant which will be shed on behalf of many for the forgiveness of sins" (not then of the "original sin"). Mark omits the specific mention of sins or sin, and so does Luke. However, both say that the blood will be shed "for many" or "for you" (Mk 14:24 and Lk 22:20, respectively). In Paul's First Letter to the Corinthians, most likely written before the Gospels, the formula "for you" is again used (1 Cor 11:24) without mention of redemption from an "original sin." The sealing of a new covenant with God (Mt 26:28; Mk 14:24; Lk 22:20; 1 Cor 11:25) refers to a passage in Jeremiah:

> The days are coming, says the Lord, when I will make a new covenant with the house of Israel and the house of Judah. It will not be like the covenant I made with their fathers the day I took them by the hand and led them forth from the land of Egypt; for they broke my covenant and I had to show myself their master, says the Lord. But this is the covenant which I will make with Israel after those days, says the Lord. I will place my law within them, and write it upon their hearts; I will be their God and they will be my people. No longer will they have to teach their friends and kinsmen how to know the Lord. All from least to greatest, shall know me, says the Lord, for I will forgive their evildoings and remember their sin no more. (Jer 31:31–34)

There is an important difference between the old covenant, which was broken, and the new one sealed by Jesus, for the first one was based on the law, on instruction, and on authority, and the new one is based on love, on what is "written in their hearts," and on what is permanently part of our innermost nature. That nature is fulfilled through love, and love is realized through sacrifice. Sin, the result of selfishness, is overcome when we give of ourselves, as shown by Jesus. We are back then to the meaning of sacrifice as such, but we are still looking for an immediate object of Jesus's sacrifice, assuming that it is not necessarily a payment for Adam's original sin or any payment at all.

Aside from the latter possibility, it is dying in the defense of truth, of opposition to the hypocrisy and self-aggrandizement of the rich and powerful, for calling them a "brood of vipers" (Mt 12:34) and for driving out of the temple those who "make God's house a market place" (Jn 2:16). Last, not least, he contradicted some of the sacred laws that either stemmed from the "hard-heartedness" of the people (Mt 19:8) or were followed mechanically as an end in themselves, unrelated to the essential love of God and the love of neighbor. Jesus constantly antagonizes the ruling class of his society. John the Baptist, who also addressed the Pharisees and Sadducees as a brood of vipers (Mt 3:7), berated King Herod Antipas for marrying his half brother's divorced wife (Mt 14:3–12). He "commanded the Jews to exercise virtue, both as righteousness toward one another, and piety towards God"[136] and had such a large following that Herod "feared lest the great influence John had over the people might put it into his power and inclination to raise a rebellion … thought it best, by putting him to death, to prevent any mischief he might cause, and to bring himself into difficulties, by sparing a man who might have him repent of it when it should be too late."[137] John, of course, never led a rebellion. He was put to death, as were innumerable defenders of the truth throughout the ages. All these were "resurrected before they died."[124,125]

But now we have to pose an important question: Is God himself sacrificing himself in the person of Jesus? Is Jesus God? In the Gospel of John the author says that the Word was God, that it became flesh and dwelt among us (Jn 1:1, 1:14). But what is the word of God if not his spirit having assumed a definable form, and are we not all Word become flesh, are we not all a manifestation of the creative spirit of God? There is a close correlation between the concept of the spirit and the concept of the word. Spirit has been forever associated with breath, but not enough attention has been paid to the fact that a word is breath processed and shaped, thus corresponding to creation by spirit. God's spirit hovers over the formless void until God utters words (Gn 1:1–3) that become physical objects or "flesh." The entire reality, including ourselves and including Jesus, is the word of God. Our human words stand apart from the results they produce as separate entities, but the word of God *is* creation—it *becomes* flesh. But if someone were to say that Jesus is the word of God not as an effect but, in his very essence, that which effects Being, I would counter that we all are, in our innermost nature, representatives of God's activity. Therefore, all of us, including Jesus, are the word of God, and there is no *qualitative* difference between him and any other creature, although there is an enormous *quantitative* difference. As an individual who has to consume resources and defend himself against a hostile environment, Jesus is still subject to our "original fault," which is supported by his own statement: "Why do you call me good? No one is good but God alone" (Mk 10:18). And yet Jesus represents the spirit of goodness in a higher degree than any creature, and thus God may be worshipped in his person. We can receive from him directions helping us on our way to Self-realization and Cosmic Consciousness, and we can follow his example as he lives and acts as a human being. He refers to his divine essence by the words "whatever you have done for these least brothers of mine you have done *for me*" (Mt 25:40, italics mine). Of course, anything we do for the least of our brothers we do for ourselves too, for our innermost nature is divine like that of Jesus.

Roger Haight, in an enlightening book, points out that a presumed qualitative difference between Jesus and ourselves contradicts the doctrine of consubstantiality with us,[138] and that only the extent of the quantitative difference makes it appear qualitative. Haight believes that in Jesus "God is so encountered that salvation is mediated by him,"[139] "a human being like all others."[140] This view has been strongly rejected by the Vatican to the point of forbidding the author to teach Catholic theology.[141]

Haight does not deny that God is a conscious person, nor have I attempted to do so. *I have only tried to show that the message of Jesus is valid even if the idea of God is reduced to an active all-pervading Principle indwelling in the entire creation, including ourselves and including Jesus.*

Viewing God as a person does not contradict that view; it only adds the additional dimension of love, not only an abstract element of love implied in the process of creative advance but also an emotional involvement with the world. The loving God gives his Son to the world. How do we understand this? The event of God giving his Son is thought by some to be symbolized by the willingness of Abraham to sacrifice his son Isaac (Gn 22:1–18). But it is impossible to impute human preferential parental feelings to God. A general would feel greater pain knowing his own son was killed in battle than he could possibly feel witnessing the death of many other young men. Yet he is willing to accept the death of his son for the greater good of his country. With God such an acceptance is absolute; there cannot be any preference at all. The very sentence "God so loved the world that he gave his only Son" (Jn 3:16) means that God's love completely exceeds any personal love because the entire world is his beloved child, a child who has to suffer to live. When we beget children, we know that we expose them to pain, because that is a necessary ingredient of life. "Giving his Son" symbolizes God's acceptance of that fact, *his exposing the world to pain and misfortune so that it may be born into being.* His truly beloved child is the living universe. He sacrifices the world to suffering and death for the greater good of life. But because God *is* in every creature as its essence, God suffers *with* every creature. This is symbolized by the suffering of Jesus, who represents God qua creature, expressing our divine essence to a greater degree than any of us.

If we assume that God is not only a loving, conscious creator but also a ruling monarch, then we add to his concept the parameters of grace, mercy, and justice. It is God's grace, then, that caused him to send his Son to effect our salvation and to die for our sins, perhaps to atone for them, God's justice thus being tempered by his mercy.

I have maintained that the sacrifice of Jesus is meaningful even if justice is not an a priori ideal given by God but only the product of the evolution of our society. Yet the fact remains that, for whatever reason, most of us have a strong feeling of guilt and responsibility, sometimes even the desire to be punished. The myth of Adam and Eve may well be an attempt to explain the painful aspects of life as a result of deserved retribution. If that be so, Jesus may conform to our mind-set by offering to accept punishment for us, by taking our desire to be punished upon himself, or at least by presenting us with an opportunity to interpret his sacrifice in such a fashion.

An argument that seeks to throw doubt upon the person of Jesus as an object of our devotion points to the fact that there were as many as sixteen crucified saviors before him, mostly mythical, and that many of his teachings may be found in Eastern religions.[142] The fact that Christian teachings can be found elsewhere certainly does not make them suspect of being wrong, and it seems to me that if Jesus, even without being an actual divine person, relived the myth of crucifixion and resurrection occurring at least sixteen times before him, it must be a myth deeply rooted in the innermost human nature and addressing the existential problems of humanity discussed here, to be taken most seriously. Jesus thus fulfilled what humanity expected, "groaning in labor pains" (Rom 8:22).

It is also noteworthy, as I already said, that the idea of obtaining eternal life by transcending one's own individuality through sacrifice is central to Christian teaching and not to that of any other major religion currently practiced.

Father, into Your Hands I Commend My Spirit

Luke 23:46
Subject: Devotion
The Vertical Beam

As a dying human being, Jesus uses words as we would use them, and therefore by the word *spirit* he must be referring to his innermost nature, the ultimate ground of all fears and desires. If he meant some immaterial remnant of his life, he would probably refer to his soul. Both words occur in different contexts in the New Testament. For example, "Behold my servant whom I have chosen ... I shall place my spirit (*pneuma*) upon him" (Mt 12:18, transliterating Is 42:1), versus, "And do not fear those who kill the body but cannot kill the soul [*psyche*]" (Mt 10:28).

The spirit that God places upon us is his own spirit, our innermost nature, the will to life, form, and love that finds its expression in various ways, beginning with the purely selfish desire for individual life and its enjoyment by the id, but progressing to the realization that life beyond one's individual limits is possible only through one's superego. That function of our personality corresponds to the spirit of Jesus of which we all partake, although it finds a more perfect manifestation in him. That spirit connects us with each other as well as with God, which is symbolized by the two beams of the cross, as I observed in the previous chapter. The connection with God is sealed by Jesus's last words: "Into your hands I commend my spirit." The sacrifice was accomplished—"finished"—for the people, but by being an act of love, it was also for God. As Bishop Fulton Sheen puts it, "The sixth word was meant for the world; the seventh word was meant for God."[143]

The love of neighbor, the love of nature, symbolized by the horizontal beam of the cross, leads necessarily to service to the Principle of Life, God in his or her most basic conceptual essence. From the recognition of that principle we may proceed to revelations or even fantasies attributing to God a personal consciousness, the humanoid emotions of love and wrath, the properties of a supreme ruler. But the insistence on such qualities, which cannot be proved, expose the entire concept of God to doubt. We should return to the basic, I believe self-evident, concept of the Principle of Life and build on it, advancing as far as we honestly can in the formation of our image of God. The basic concept is a spirit to which we are dedicated, a dedication expressed by the Seventh Word from the cross. It was expressed earlier in a Psalm (Ps 31:6) and has later become part of the Night Prayer of the religious.[144]

Our relationship with others and with the entirety of our environment—that is, all our moral and ethical concepts, that horizontal beam of our existence—are irrevocably tied to the vertical beam, to our essential identity with the Principle of Life. Our spirit is in God's hands whether we know it or not, and by placing it in his hands in prayer, we bring that fact to our consciousness.

Some argument will always be made that morality is a product of utility, namely the maintenance of a society satisfactory for its members based on reciprocity. I believe I have shown that such a view is inadequate, that morality serves, through identification with others, living beyond ourselves. It is also impossible to explain our love of nature, which exceeds any utilitarian attachment to the earth, our products of art, and even of science without the element of love transcending our individual being. Science certainly has practical applications, and technology has even more, but neither is conceivable without a creative impulse—*eros,* if you will—driving scientists and inventors. Of course, if we believe that all these efforts satisfy our innermost nature, we admit to a higher form of utility, for what could be more useful to us than such satisfaction?

Earlier, I quoted the gospel of Mary Magdalene in order to define three entities constituting the human person: the *spirit,* which is the common moving principle; the *soul,* meaning not some immaterial remnant surviving the body, but the psycho-physical stuff wrapped around the principle; and *nous,* the *mind* acting on behalf of the spirit, mediating between our innermost nature and our thinking and acting, often mistaken, personality. The spirit, our innermost essence, already belongs to God by virtue of its identity with him, but our mind needs to remind us of that fact, inducing us to confess to that identity consciously, as Jesus does at the moment of his death.

It is appropriate in this context to review the existing social systems and their relation to the spirit that constitutes our innermost nature. Such a relation must exist, for it concerns of necessity all aspects of our life. Gandhi saw that clearly. He said, "To see the universal and all-pervading Spirit of Truth face to face, one must be able to love the meanest creature as oneself. And a man who aspires after that cannot afford to keep out of any field of life. That is why my devotion to Truth has drawn me into the field of politics; and I can say without the slightest hesitation, and yet in all humility, that those who say that religion has nothing to do with politics do not know what religion means."[145]

Any attention to political systems in existence throughout history will show that whereas economic conditions and population pressures, as well as the desire for power, can always be found as moving forces behind events and conditions, they alone are insufficient to effect change, that people need ideals to justify their political views and their dedication to either the status quo or a change thereof. Such ideals transcending individual lives and individual physical needs are religious in a wider sense.

Since ancient times divinity has been attributed to earthly rulers: the Roman emperors, the emperors of Japan, and the emperors of China, for example. Although not themselves divine, the European monarchs were thought to be divinely ordained, and as their attributes of power, mercy, wisdom, and justice were transferred to the concept of God, the supreme ruler of the universe, these qualities reflected upon them as divine gifts.

Paul's statement that all authority should be obeyed since all authority is from God (Rom 13:1) has helped to reinforce the belief in the divine right of rulers, tyrants though they may be. It is usually overlooked that Paul contradicted himself in opposing the purportedly divine authority of the emperor and preaching Christianity, for which he was beheaded.

The atheist social theory of communism professes an inevitable dialectic process based on economic factors, and yet it is clear from reading the *Communist Manifesto* that the coming dictatorship of the proletariat is *good*. In his introduction to the *Communist Manifesto*, Francis P. Randall says that the "highly romantic sense of social wrong, and the consequent highly Romantic drive toward social justice, which Marx and Engels shared to a high degree, are the ethical and emotional bases of any socialist movement."[146] Not only is this ideal of social justice religious in a wider sense, but the elements of the foreseen revolution correspond, as Bertrand Russell pointed out, to a Christian religious pattern: Marx being the Messiah, the rule of the proletariat the kingdom of God, and the capitalists the Devil.[147] Similarly, the allegedly a-religious National Socialism, taking foot in economically depressed post–World War I Germany, is not only full of Romantic concepts such as "blood and soil" but revives the biblical concept of a chosen people, and here again the Führer assumes the role of the Messiah, the failed "Tausendjähriges Reich" that of the kingdom of God, and the Jews that of the Devil.

These are examples of how political movements, obviously conditioned by material needs, require the spark of spirit to be activated.

In July 2012, the *Los Angeles Times* published an article contending that many of the world's civil conflicts arise in nations where runaway population growth has created huge pools of young people who are exposed to unemployment and lack of opportunity.[148] The author describes the plight of the youth in Afghanistan that prompts them to join the Taliban, a religious extremist organization. The material advantages offered by such an association are inseparably linked to the promise of paradise, especially if one gives his life to the common cause.

In Islam, the association of economic factors with spiritual stimuli goes back to the very beginning when "Mohammed unified the Bedouins for the first time in their history and thus made it possible for them, as a potentially powerful military group, to yoke together their economic need and their religious faith in an overwhelming drive out of the desert."[149] Several hundred years later extreme poverty in the growing population of Europe and the prevailing system of inheritance that excluded all but the eldest son gave material substance to the religious zeal of the Crusaders, reminiscent of today's combination of economic and religious factors in the conflict between Western democracies and the fanatic adherents of Islam in the Near East.[150]

The democratic ideals of the Western powers are of particular interest to us since they dominate our political concepts as a quasi religion. Our forefathers, oppressed by "taxation without representation," having to pay dearly for imported goods such as their tea, could not revolt without a spiritual spark. This was provided by the idea of allegedly God-given human rights put forth in our Declaration of Independence.

The text of this document is indeed inspiring, yet the "human rights" proclaimed therein cannot withstand rational scrutiny. The right to liberty and pursuit of happiness is certainly not inalienable, for it is severely restricted whenever it interferes with the well-being of others or the interests of the state. The right to life is interfered with by the very country proclaiming it by capital punishment and by sending men and women to war to kill and be killed, and by accepting or even deliberately causing civilian casualties in such wars. The unborn child, in the early stages of its development, is in the United States constitutionally excluded from the right to life. Furthermore, this right to life with which we are allegedly endowed by our Creator is eventually revoked by that very Creator in 100 percent of individuals. Since everyone wants to live and to have his way—and since no one pursues unhappiness—life, liberty, and the pursuit of happiness are, properly called, human needs rather than human rights. *It is to satisfy these needs that civil rights are granted within a society.*

In 1790, Edmund Burke, horrified by the excesses of the French Revolution that was inspired by the idea of the Rights of Man, expressed the view that no right can exist if it is incompatible with virtue, and, in 1840, Jeremy Bentham argued that it is wrong to regard liberty, equality, and justice as ends in themselves and not as means to public happiness.[151] He says, as I have, that the pursuit of happiness is not a natural right but a natural inclination, that "Every thing is referred to pleasures or to pains" and that one should "prefer that which promises the greater sum of good."[152] But in a state where a minority of the population is enslaved by a well-to-do majority, such a situation may well amount to "the greater sum of good" if only the pleasures and pains of that state's citizens are taken into account. We know that such a situation is morally wrong and can be justified only by fallacious arguments. To be valid, the principle of *utility*, which Bentham defines as "that principle which approves or disapproves of every action whatever, according to the tendency which it appears to have to augment or diminish the happiness of the party whose interest is in question: or, what is the same thing in other words, to promote or oppose that happiness,"[153] must therefore reach deeper and satisfy our common innermost nature. Neither a priori inalienable rights nor transient pleasures and pains of a majority may contradict that *supreme utility*. In the service to our innermost nature, which implies mutual respect and understanding, we must introduce *civil rights*, alienable whenever they come in conflict with their original purpose. A perusal of the Universal Declaration of Human Rights adopted by the United Nations General Assembly on December 10, 1948, and available online, will show that wherever a concept is not too vague to be defined in legal terms, such as "freedom" and "dignity," it refers to a civil right, often corresponding to one in our own Bill of Rights. The same applies to the Declaration of the Rights of Man and of Citizens by the National Assembly of France.[154] The United Nations Declaration deserves our wholehearted support, and if it pleases the world to refer to it as a list of *human rights,* so be it, but I believe that the original concept of inalienable human rights is false and thus must lead to a basic misunderstanding of the essence of the laws of society.

Unfortunately, another irrational concept is introduced as the foundation of "human rights" and the legislation derived therefrom, namely the maxim that "all men are created equal." In the context of a revolt against a feudal society or against racial discrimination, the concept of equality is understandable, meaning that there should be no privilege of cast, that the son of a nobleman should not be viewed as worth more than a son of a peasant or a laborer, and that racial or national origin per se should not determine a person's worth. The same applies to discrimination based on sex. All such discrimination is wicked, but unfortunately it is still alive and well in many instances and as such should be combated wherever it is found.

We are all equal in our contribution to Being because the immensity of the plenum of Being in the universe makes any individual contribution shrink to an infinitesimal size. But clearly, considered in the framework of human society, men are not created equal in their circumstances or ability. In 1932, J. B. S. Haldane published a fine book expounding on that obvious inequality and its consequences.[155] Nevertheless, different social systems continue to misinterpret the concept of equality and attempt to fit it into their view of the function of society. The capitalist system proclaims that everyone is equal before the law and is possessed of the same human and civil rights, yet it does not impose upon a government the obligation to assist anyone in the exercise of those rights. Thus, everyone is equal in his right to compete and to make money without interference by any authority.

It is that kind of a capitalist society that Marx envisioned when he predicted a communist takeover. The Universal Declaration of

Human Rights provides for the right to help by the state (Article 25), but such provision is conspicuously absent from the United States Bill of Rights. The communist systems recognize the inequality of individuals by their maxim "from everyone according to his ability, to everyone according to his needs," but they have repeatedly attempted to overcome that admitted inequality by forceful methods. Thus, inequality in ability and competence was denied during the Cultural Revolution in China and under the Pol Pot regime in Cambodia, when every citizen was forced to perform all tasks without regard to ability or training. For a short time after the Russian Revolution, everyone received the same salary for whatever work they performed, a system called *uravnilovka*, "equalization," soon abolished as unproductive.

I would suggest that instead of the deceptive concept of universal *equality* we consider the concept of universal *identity*, already repeatedly introduced above. It is the realization that in our innermost nature we all desire life in harmony with others and that in that respect we share our identity with the Creator, be he or she a principle, a moving force, or a person endowed with conscious love. It then corresponds to our innermost desire to share our fortunes with others and to grant them civil rights *that eliminate or at least ameliorate the inequalities with which we were created.* Thus, whereas certain laws must apply to everyone, regardless of their economic status, intelligence, or racial origin, others, while limiting a citizen's rights and privileges, must provide means of compensation. For example, although a person with inadequate vision must be prohibited from driving a car, provisions must be made for adequate transportation for such a person, and if an individual with below-average intelligence cannot work in certain occupations, it is up to society to provide suitable employment opportunities for him or her. Under such a system people are neither forcefully equalized nor left to fend for themselves when presented with "equal opportunity." Affirmative Action was introduced to ameliorate the inequalities resulting from centuries of discrimination based on race. But similar action should also be applied whenever remediable inequalities exist because of differences between humans. Because of these differences the system cannot be based on an alleged complete inborn *equality* but rather on an *identity* that not only interdicts any racial or national discrimination but also calls for help whenever needed for whatever reason.

Not only is *identity* a more correct term to describe the relationship of various people, but it also implies a bond through a common nature, whereas *equality* denotes a number of entities placed side by side, not necessarily connected.

The realization of identity extends not only to other people but to all creatures and to the entirety of nature. There are no God-given animal rights, nor is there a God-given mandate to serve the environment. But the realization of the essential identity of all created beings leads us to serve other people, support other creatures, and preserve our natural environment. That preservation thus becomes a spiritual task far beyond any utilitarian advantage.

The symbolism of the cross with its horizontal and vertical components is restated in the symbolism of the Holy Eucharist. By receiving the body and blood of the Lord, we affirm our unity with the Creative Principle manifested in Jesus, and we affirm our unity with others simultaneously. Through that affirmation we "commend our spirit into the hands of God," as Jesus did.

SECTION 3

Thoughts on the Beatitudes

Matthew 5:3–11

The considerations related to the Seven Last Words prepare us for a better understanding of the beatitudes, the most essential and, in praxis, most ignored teachings of Jesus. More than any other pronouncements they preach unity with the world around us and with the all-pervading Principle of Life. *Blessedness is Cosmic Consciousness.*

Blessed Are the Poor in Spirit, for Theirs Is the Kingdom of Heaven

Blessed Are They Who Hunger and Thirst for Righteousness, for They Will Be Satisfied

The first problem posed by this beatitude is the definition of the *kingdom of heaven*. Many would interpret it as the paradise expecting the righteous after death or God's rule on earth after the resurrection of the dead. We may certainly believe that, perhaps even derive it from the text of some of the Scriptures, but if we believe that God is present in all things, we must also assume that his kingdom is everywhere, that it may well expand its influence, but that it cannot come to us because it is already here. I shall maintain that this interpretation of the kingdom of heaven, which, by definition, can be equated to the kingdom of God, fits better into Jesus's parables than the one of a future state. In a number of allegorical representations (Mt 13) Jesus defines the kingdom of heaven in ways that correspond to the recognition of its presence here and now. According to Jesus's own words the parable of the sower (Mt 13:3–8) refers to individuals with "knowledge of the mysteries of the kingdom of heaven" (Mt 13:11) "in whom the word bears fruit" (Mt 13:23). The parables of the mustard seed and the yeast (Mt 13:31–33) compare the growth of the former and the spread through the dough of the latter with the growth of the kingdom of heaven. They could be taken as symbols for the gradual spread of the kingdom throughout the world, but Jesus's explanation of the parable of the sower justifies its application to the nature of man gradually becoming aware of his divine essence. The parables of the treasure buried in the field and found by a person who then buys the field (Mt 13:44) and of the precious pearl that one acquires at a high cost (Mt 13:45–46) again imply the acquisition of the awareness of the kingdom by the individual. Its presence in the world is finally referred to in the parables of the weeds among the wheat (Mt 13:24–30) and the bad fishes among the good (Mt 13:47–48). All these passages indicate that the kingdom is present now, although it will be complete only at "the end of the age" (Mt 13:49).

Jesus's statement "The Kingdom of God is within you" (Lk 17:20–21) or, as it is translated in the New American Bible, "among you" also denotes the presence of the kingdom here and now. *A New Catholic Commentary on Holy Scripture* says that the term *among you* is preferable because Jesus speaks to Pharisees.[156] I disagree; the kingdom of God, our innermost essence, is present in everyone, no matter how obscured it may be. This is said even more clearly in the gospel of Thomas: "The Kingdom is inside you, and it is outside you. When you know yourself you will be known and you will know that you are the child of the living Father."[157] Another quote in the same book reads, "The Kingdom of the Father is spread out over the whole earth and the people do not see it."[158]

Joseph Bracken expresses the same thought when he says, "The Kingdom of God is a network of relationships that have stood the test of time and that in retrospect have given meaning and value, not simply to human history but to the whole course of cosmic evolution from the Big Bang onward."[159] He believes then that the kingdom of God is present now but still develops toward greater prevalence through the "collective power of good."[160]

Whitehead equated the kingdom of heaven to the consequent nature of God. He writes, "The consequent nature of God is the fulfillment of his experience by his reception of the multiple freedom of actuality into the harmony of his own actualization … This is God in his function as Kingdom of Heaven."[161] Whitehead's thought implies that God will integrate all experiences into a perfect whole at some point. Thus the consequent nature of God is with us today but still moving toward completion.

John B. Cobb Jr. elucidates Whitehead's concepts, again viewing the kingdom of heaven as a divine presence moving toward completion of "historical hope."[162]

Historical hope is also the foundation of Teilhard de Chardin's Omega Point, a creative center, present from the beginning of creation as a goal of final harmony. It involves "not only a conservation but an exaltation of the elements by convergence,"[163] "when Christ appears above the clouds, doing nothing but manifesting the slowly accomplished metamorphosis of the hearts of the mass of humanity."[164] Some progress toward this ideal can be seen in present-day society. We no longer consider other races inferior, and we accept their cultures as valid alternatives to ours. Individuals of different sexual orientation are accepted as equally valuable members of society. In political life, the European Union is an attempt to abolish national hostilities under preservation of national identities, and the United Nations tries to accomplish this on an even greater scale. As the foregoing of revenge, discussed earlier, such moves toward integration have not only an obvious material benefit but also an enormous metaphysical significance. They all represent progress toward the "Omega Point," or, if you will, manifestations of the "Consequent Nature of God." Will such progress continue? We do not know. It is certainly a dream as old as our civilization, expressed by Isaiah, who speaks of a coming age when "the wolf shall be the guest of the lamb and the leopard shall lie down with the kid ... for the earth shall be filled with the knowledge of the Lord, as water covers the sea" (Is 11:6–9). But since Being in general must be manifested by particular being involving some opposition of individual members, such progress can proceed only in an asymptotic fashion.

A conviction that such completion will ever be realized is not needed for finding the kingdom of heaven within and around us. In the words of Teilhard de Chardin, the omnipresence of God defined as his kingdom is reflected in all creatures "as the sun in the many pieces of a broken mirror."[165] And yet, we cannot realize that kingdom within ourselves unless we are trying to bring it about in the world, even if we do not succeed. According to Edward Schillebeeckx "the hermeneutics of the Kingdom of God, consists especially in making the world a better place. Only in this way will I be able to discover what the Kingdom of God means."[166] And John Cobb writes regarding the New Testament that "it presupposes that we are capable of finding our greatest satisfaction in the assurance that we contribute beyond ourselves, ultimately to the Kingdom itself."[167]

All these thoughts agree with the gist of Jesus's parables implying that the kingdom of heaven is with us here and now, within us and among us, but that it cannot be realized without our conscious contribution. Its essence is a "creative advance into novelty." Bucke equated this kingdom, as presented by Jesus, with Cosmic Consciousness.[168] I would modify that view by saying that Cosmic

Consciousness is the grasping of the omnipresence of God and thus an entry into the kingdom rather than the kingdom itself. *The kingdom of heaven is the presence of God (or the all-pervading Principle of Life) within and without.*

The second problem posed by this first beatitude is its interpretation as either "the *poor in spirit* are blessed," or "the *poor* are blessed in spirit." Since Luke's quote is simply "Blessed are the Poor," (Lk 6:20) even followed by a threat—"Woe to you who are rich, for you received your consolation!" (Lk 6:24)—and since the author of the gospel of Thomas also quotes, "Blessed are you, the poor, for yours is the Kingdom of Heaven,"[169] the second meaning should be acceptable. Furthermore, Jesus's brother James, who should have known his teacher's mind, praises the poor and predicts perdition for the rich (Jas 1:9–11, 5:1–6). Jesus obviously was railing against social injustice, and against abuses by the priestly class and the well-to-do. This was an important reason for his execution and possibly for James's as well.[170] But a social reformer does not consider the poor blessed; he or she would advocate anything to help them out of their misery. One might think that Jesus thought the poor and the disenfranchised blessed because he foresaw an impending change of the social order, a revolution similar to the "rule of the proletariat" prophesied by Marx. Reza Aslan in his best-selling book about the historical Jesus favors such an interpretation.[171] But the parables about the kingdom of heaven are incompatible with it. It is remarkable that the author of Matthew's gospel, while trying to prove that Jesus is a descendant of David and the Messiah promised by the prophets,[172] paints an entirely spiritual picture of his kingdom. He speaks of a spiritual, not a material, fulfillment of God's promises. If the "poor" are to be the ones who partake therein, they must be those people who are not concerned with material goods. *The abjectly poor are not blessed* and deserve our help, not only because misery is bad but also because they too have to be primarily concerned with food and shelter and are more likely to resort to violence than to prayer. In hard economic times, crime rates go up, not down.

According to all three Synoptic Gospels (Mk 10:21; Mt 19:21; Lk 18:22), Jesus asks the rich man to sell his goods to help the poor. It is obvious that he does not consider the misery of poverty a blessing but rather its acceptance as a spiritual attitude, the lack of concern with material possessions.

Meister Eckhart writes, "Now, there are two kinds of poverty. One is the external poverty, and it is good and very praiseworthy for the man who takes it up willingly out of love of our Lord Jesus Christ who himself accepted it in his earthly life … In addition, there is another poverty, an internal poverty, that is to be understood as being meant in the words of our Lord when he says: 'Blessed are the poor in spirit.'"[173] Meister Eckhart continues to say that the poor in spirit "want nothing, know nothing and have nothing," which can mean only that they are not beholden to any *object* of want, knowledge, or possession, and that they dedicate themselves entirely to God. That would involve, of course, serving the creative advance into novelty, yet not serving it for individual material gain. God too ceases to be an object but is realized as the essence of one's innermost nature. Thus, later in the same sermon, Meister Eckhart says, "Poverty of the spirit exists only when the individual stands apart from God and his works in such a manner, that God, wanting to work in the soul, is always himself the site where He works." He adds, "In this very situation, in this state of poverty Man attains the eternal Being which he was and is now and will be forever."[174]

Matthew Fox classifies this beatitude and Eckhart's sermon as taking the path of "Letting Go," the "Via Negativa."[175] But I prefer to view this "poverty of the spirit" more as a realization of our essence than an abandonment of individual existence, a state I intend to address in discussing the vision of God. It is not enough to abandon the concern for worldly possessions. Our actions must be directed toward serving the kingdom of God, and that requires dedication, not just being poor but being a beggar, craving the good in the world.

Therefore, Meister Eckhart has also combined the two beatitudes I am discussing here (Mt 5:3 and Mt 5:6). He quotes: "Blessed are the poor and those who thirst for righteousness."[176] He sees that pursuit of righteousness as self-fulfillment, acting without an ulterior motive such as pleasing a superior power. He writes, "Thus, as God works without a Why and does not know a Why—entirely in the same manner as God acts, thus also acts the righteous man without a Why; and thus as life lives for its own sake and seeks no Why for the sake of which it lives, in the same manner the righteous man knows no Why for the sake of which he would do something."[177] In acting for the sake of my innermost nature, for the sake of the kingdom of God within me, without an external why, *I will be satisfied whether I succeed or not.* But if we hunger for justice, we should seek justice in society as a hungry man seeks food. We cannot watch injustices with equanimity; we must act. We are back to the fact that we cannot realize the kingdom of heaven within ourselves if we do not attempt to serve it through action in our environment—in other words outside ourselves, hopeless as it may be. I shall return to this subject in discussing the last two beatitudes.

The poor in spirit then are those who put aside concerns about objects of possession and power for the sake of the kingdom of heaven, a process involving Self-realization and Cosmic Consciousness. It is a state they beg for in accordance with their innermost nature and that they realize not only by their attitude but also by their pursuit of righteousness.

My soul yearns and pines for the courts of the Lord. My heart and flesh cry out for the living God (Ps 84:2).

2

Blessed Are the Meek, for They Will Inherit the Land

This beatitude echoes verse 11 of Psalm 37, which in the New American Bible is translated as "the poor shall possess the land, will delight in great prosperity." The Hebrew word used there is *anavim,* which, in other passages, designates "poverty of the spirit" or humbleness such as in Isaiah 61:1: "He has sent me to bring glad tidings to the lowly (*anavim*)" and Zephaniah 2:3: "Seek the Lord, all you humble (*anavim*) of the earth." In the book of Numbers it is written, "Now Moses himself was by far the meekest (*meode anav*) man on the face of the earth" (Nm 12:3). The Jewish scholar Jennifer Ross cites these and multiple other examples,[178] and the New American Bible in the commentary to Psalm 22:27, "the poor (*anavim*) will eat their fill," confirms that the meaning of that word "came to include the humble, pious and devout."

Thus, the same people must be meant in this beatitude as in the one first discussed, except that there the *anavim* are promised the kingdom of heaven and here the land. How are we to interpret that statement?

"The meek are not going to inherit the earth," says a character in Barbara Kingsolver's *Poisonwood Bible.* Indeed, this character's observations lead her to believe that the meek and defenseless are invariably oppressed and, when they dare to speak up, violently eliminated. The cataclysmic second coming of Christ and the eventual establishment of a peaceable kingdom of God on earth can certainly be accepted on faith only, even though, as I mentioned above, there are some signs of mankind evolving toward a greater unity and a firmer establishment of peace. Several authors whom I quoted in the section on the first beatitude lend hope for the future.

But all such optimism is subject to uncertainty, and we are still faced with individuals and groups wielding secular power and promoting cycles of violence in most of the world. I shall try to show the validity of the Christian doctrine apart from hopeful promises applied to the present world with all its persistent violence and still existing rampant abuse of power.

What does *inheritance* mean? When someone in my family dies, I might inherit a house. But if I value the house only as a financial asset and perhaps as a shelter, and do not take loving care of it, then even though I have the power to sell it or even raze it to the ground, I inherited only the house's shell, not its entire value. A person working for me, caring for the house, being emotionally attached to it, enjoying and beautifying the grounds is the true beneficiary of my inheritance. If I delight in the beauty of the "amber fields of grain," the "purple mountains' majesty," in the perfume of the forest on a summer day, in the gentle wind caressing my skin or even in the majesty of a violent storm, in the depth of the sky, be it blue with wandering clouds or black studded with stars, I have certainly a more profound use of the land than someone who grows grain simply for profit, cuts or sells timber, or harnesses the wind to make electricity. Of course, one using the land for profit is never barred from seeing its beauty, but the idea of its objective utility may get in his or her way.

I inherit the land not by acquiring it but by being accepted into it—by embracing it, not by grasping it. In the words of Martin Buber, "Between you and the World there is mutual giving; you say Thou to her and give yourself to her and she gives herself to you … and she leads you by the joy of her arrivals and the sorrow of her departures toward that Thou within which the lines of relationships, the parallel ones, intersect. She does not help you to stay alive but she helps you to anticipate eternity."[179]

Such an I-thou relationship must involve humbleness, for it is lost as soon as I stand above the land and lord over it in an I-it relationship. In that case there is not a merging but a connection, and a connection can always be broken. It is an uncertain inheritance.

There is another way to live consistent with the ordinary concept of meekness, yet it is misguided. It is the attempt to belong without understanding that only by serving life through love can we realize the identity of our innermost nature with the Principle of Life and thus open the door to Cosmic Consciousness. This misguided way of belonging is conformation to habits and prejudices of the crowd for the sake of improving social standing, such as joining others in shouting, "Crucify him! Crucify him!" (Lk 23:21). This type of meekness, possessed by the masses, conforms to what Heidegger called "das Man"[180] and is not meant by the beatitude discussed here. "Das Man" is meek before society; *the individual approaching Cosmic Consciousness is meek before life, meek before God.* Humbleness and meekness before God involve a firm, if not violent, stand against the injustices in the world, as I have already said and as I shall reiterate under the heading of the beatitude to be discussed last.

Blessed Are the Clean of Heart, for They Will See God

The meaning of the word *heart* in biblical Hebrew implies more than the emotional disposition generally denoted by this term. David Steinberg has listed the various metaphoric meanings of it in the Bible with the conclusion that there the term *heart* denotes the entire mental and emotional makeup of a person.[181]

That makeup consists of the psycho-physical stuff surrounding our innermost nature, the will to live—pure Being energizing and generating individual being. To realize our innermost essence in its purest form we must give up that mental and physical individuality, we must proceed to the heart of the heart. Brought to consciousness, such a state is equal to realizing our identity with the ground of Being, the Principle of Life, equal to "seeing God" within oneself, fully realizing one's identity with the essence of the universe. Such giving up of individuality equals death in the created world. If we could accomplish giving up all adversarial function of our person, we could not stay alive, for, as already said, we need to compete with our environment, fight off microorganisms, and often be in conflict with other individuals. Mentally too we are necessarily tuned to self-defense, all love for others being "imperfect" in that regard.

Therefore, while we are still alive, which God, the Principle of Life, wants us to be, we can be privy to only a partial vision of him, such as one achieved by *poverty of spirit* and *humbleness*. The outer limit of these virtues is a complete abandoning of self. The ancient biblical statement that no man can see God and live (Ex 33:20) is thus validated. There are interesting examples of actual experiences of such self-abandonment.

A person identified as C. M. C. by Bucke says, "I felt myself going, losing myself. Then I was terrified, but with a sweet terror. I was losing my consciousness, my identity, but was powerless to hold myself."[182] Another individual, M. C. L., says, "This grew until I found myself rising and expanding into the Infinite, being diffused and lost therein, and the mind and body reeled. Feeling myself falling I exclaimed: 'The vision is too much! I cannot look upon the face of God and live! Father in heaven, it is enough!' And the voice answered. I sank on my bed and slept like a child."[183]

These people describe an at least temporary state of Self-realization that we might call "purity of heart," a view of one's innermost Self and its identity with the infinite ground of Being. I am aware of two similar experiences described in the world literature: one by Dostoyevsky in the novel *The Demons*, the other by Somerset Maugham in the *The Razor's Edge*.

In *The Demons*, the character Kiriloff says this:

> There are seconds, only about five or six in a row when you feel the presence of eternal harmony perfectly achieved. This is not an earthly phenomenon. I am not saying that it is from heaven, all I mean is that a man in his terrestrial state cannot bear it. One has to change physically and die. The feeling is clear and indisputable. It is as if one perceives the entirety

of nature and says: 'Yes, this is truth, this is good.' You do not forgive anything to anyone because there is nothing to forgive. Not that you love, that is above and beyond love! The most terrifying thing is that absolute clarity and joy! Five more seconds and your soul cannot stand it and must perish. In those moments I pass my whole life and for them I would give my life because they are worth it. To endure it for ten seconds one must change physically. I think man would stop procreating; what good are children, what good progress once the ultimate goal has been achieved.[184]

In *The Razor's Edge*, the hero, Larry Darrell, reports this experience:

... a strange sensation, a tingling that arose from my feet and traveled up my head, and I felt as though I was suddenly released from my body and as pure spirit partook in a loveliness I never before conceived. I had a sense that knowledge more than human possessed me, so that everything that was confused was clear and everything that had perplexed me was explained. I was so happy that it was pain and I struggled to release myself from it, for I felt that if it lasted a moment longer I would die; and yet it was such a rapture that I was ready to die rather than forgo it ... When I came to myself I was exhausted and trembling. I fell asleep.[185]

Dostoyevsky's novel was written in 1871 and 1872, almost thirty years before Bucke's book was published, and it could be that Dostoyevsky relates his own experience in Kiriloff's words, perhaps a phenomenon of an epileptic aura (Kiriloff's interlocutor asks if he, Kiriloff, by any chance suffers from the "falling sickness"). The similarity to the cases reported by Bucke is remarkable.

I have no way of knowing whether Maugham ever experienced "Cosmic Consciousness" himself or if he heard about this experience as part of his study of Hinduism.[186] In any event, he certainly understood it.

The promise to actually see God because of a clean heart is found only in the Sermon on the Mount, and seeing him is also referred to in First John: "No one has ever seen God. Yet, if we love one another, God remains in us and his love is brought to perfection in us" (1 Jn 4:12). This is then the first step toward giving up one's self and thus obtaining a partial vision of God. Perhaps, in our final hour, we all may be blessed by being granted a full vision: "Beloved, we are God's children now; what we shall be has not yet been revealed. We know that when it is revealed we shall be like him for we shall see him as he is" (1 Jn 3:2).

4

Blessed Are Those Who Mourn,
for They Will Be Comforted

The corresponding quote in the gospel of Luke (Lk 6:21) is "Blessed are you who are now weeping, for you will laugh," and unlike Matthew's version, it is followed by a threat: "Woe to you who laugh now, for you will grieve and weep" (Lk 6:25). Both statements refer to reward and punishment in an afterlife or a future world.

Common sense will accept the notion of a reward for suffering. A punishment for having been happy, on the other hand, seems repugnant. And yet, if we truly believe in compensation in a better world, then such compensation should be more generous for those who suffered than for those who did not. Hence, the self-infliction of deprivation and pain by some religious individuals. But, according to the gospel of Matthew (Mt 25:40), Jesus bases his final judgment not on the amount of misery or happiness one has been subject to, as Luke indicates in the quote cited above, as well as in his story about the rich man and Lazarus (Lk 16:19–31), but on works of love. "Whatever you have done for these least brothers of mine, you have done for me" is essential to the message of Jesus, and therefore worth bringing up over and over again.

Numerous hermits and flagellants have chosen deprivation and pain instead of charity as a way to please God, a method that may be just as self-centered as the accumulation of wealth and power. I shall not presume to interpret the motivation of those people or their ultimate influence on the course of the world. I must also add that asceticism, the voluntary abandonment of luxuries, is different from the self-infliction of pain for its own sake.

This is not a study of the judgmental or compensatory activity of a conscious deity, although its existence is by no means denied. *This book is an attempt to impute a meaning to the words of Jesus as they may relate to man not being cared for by an omnipotent God yet conscious of his or her basic and absolutely necessary involvement with cosmic life and with randomly distributed evil.* What comfort can be found under such circumstances?

Common sense tells us that mourning and suffering may enhance our appreciation of the good things in life, but I believe that the ultimate comfort of mourning and mishaps lies deeper.

In speaking about the Fourth Word from the cross, "my God, why have you forsaken me," I proposed that acceptance of adversity is needed to validate our love of life, the forever moving and changing essence of the universe. I shall now go further by saying that the comfort of suffering lies not only in the acceptance of life as it is but also *in the acceptance of ourselves as living beings, as building stones of life.*

We tend to consider our person as one thing and whatever happens to us, our fate, as another. But in reality, these two things cannot be separated. *"Yo soy yo y mi circunstancia"* (I am I and my circumstance), says Jose Ortega y Gasset[187] and somewhere else: *"El pasado no está allí, en su fecha, sino aquí en mí. El pasado soy yo—se entiende, mi vida"* (The past is not there, at its place in time, but here, in me. The past is I—meaning my life).[188] Whatever happens to me becomes mine, part of the person I am. *Without my good and bad experiences I would have no life. I owe my defined existence to them, and through them I become an integral part of cosmic life. Thus I transcend my spatial and temporal limits and fulfill the goal of my innermost nature. That is the greatest comfort of mourning I can receive, aside from any compensation In this world or the next.* My view is supported by the 58th Logion in the Gospel of Thomas; "Yeshua said: Blessed are those who have undergone ordeals. They have entered into life."[189]

Mourning is not limited to pain inflicted upon us. It is also the sum of regrets, of missed opportunities, of wrong and selfish decisions. Such wrongful decisions may affect the limited goals of my "id" or my "ego," but they may also affect my innermost nature seeking utmost harmony with others, seeking service to life in general. In that case, my superego suffers the offense that I perceive as sin.

"Sin is *behovabil*," says Julian of Norwich, using a Middle English word variously translated as *appropriate, necessary, expedient,* or *inevitable,* "nor can it be known except by the pain that is caused by it. And this pain, it is something for a time, as I see it, because it purges and forces us to know ourselves and ask for mercy."[190] *Mercy* usually means forgiveness by a judge, but if such a judge does not exist, it must mean an acceptance of myself as a forever seeking and erring agent of life.

But before such an acceptance of myself becomes possible, I must know what I accept. I must perceive my sin in its true significance and sincerely resolve not to commit it again. Otherwise, my realization is a hollow one. The full awareness of my sin brings with it the pain of injury to my innermost nature, but it also brings the knowledge that through my wrongful act I have participated in life, its ugly side, and that the resulting pain is a necessary part of it. That is one comfort that I can find in the remembrance of my sin. For most of us, however, such comfort cannot completely eliminate the feeling of guilt, the result of a necessary but still negative contribution to the plenum of life. I shall address this problem in the section about the next beatitude.

Of course, the final significance of any act, be it good or evil according to its immediate appearance, remains uncertain, for any event contains both aspects, and its long-range effects are impossible to know. Therefore, in judging myself, I have to rely on whatever system of moral laws has been given to me, be it common decency, religion, or conscience. But the ultimate arbiter is my service to the greatest possible unity and harmony of all beings. Without such service rooted in love, or at least in an image of love, all morality is a mere shell, or worse, self-defeating.

The joy of knowing that through pain and sin, once we have seen them in their true significance, we become part of the cosmic life, that we are accepted in the family of beings, accepted back in the sea of life from which we emerged, is symbolized by the story of the return of the prodigal son (Lk 15:11–32). In Luke's text, emphasis is placed on the joy of the father who welcomes the "resurrection" of his son. But does it not seem that the joy of the returning son must be greater than that of the faithful son who has always done what was expected of him? Furthermore, if our Father is God who dwells within us, then the Father's joy is our own joy caused by having gone through the obstacles that life put before us.

There is another positive side of our mourning, another service to life we must not forget. It is the ability to convey our experience to the generations to come, to tell them what we have done, where we have failed, and how such failures can be avoided. New life is growing around us waiting for our input and for nourishment from us, as new growth eagerly absorbs the nutrients from fallen leaves.

5

Blessed Are the Merciful, for They Will Obtain Mercy

In discussing the First Word of Jesus on the cross, I have maintained that we are unable to correctly judge the individual responsibility of others, and that, furthermore, such judging interferes with our achieving unity with them and thus with life in general. Under the heading of the last beatitude discussed, I said that acceptance of our own sins equals the acceptance of life in the form closest to us, namely of ourselves. But where such errors involve breakage of what we consider moral maxims, we cannot rid ourselves of the specter of guilt. I suggested also that the concept of guilt may have developed in the course of our social evolution because of the need of some individuals to defend themselves against the selfish acts of others, and that the image of God as a perfect judge has been derived from the concept of a ruling terrestrial individual. Whether this is true or not, the concepts of justice and guilt are deeply ingrained in our view of the world and in the view of ourselves. Transgressions cause us to suffer pangs of conscience and to desire forgiveness.

Forgiving myself may be at times more difficult than forgiving others because we can more easily explain their actions as a result of causative factors than we can our own, being unshakably convinced that we possess a free will. We cannot help but feel responsible for our sins. The reason it seems easier for people to judge others than to judge themselves, why wicked individuals seem to be perfectly comfortable in spite of leading condemnable lives, is a strong defense mechanism permitting us to suppress the awareness of our faults and failures. But once we fully realize them, they must seem more glaring to us than all the misdeeds of others, and the process of accepting them is indeed painful. It may be that such a full realization awaits us at the time of death, if not in an afterlife.

The seat of conscience, the realization of guilt in addition to the realization of failure, must be seated in the *nous*, in the mind, which mediates between our innermost nature and the "psycho-physical stuff" enveloping it.

It is often overlooked that the desire for forgiveness is as selfish as the self-centeredness that has caused our transgressions to begin with. I, as an individual, want to be looked upon favorably by others, I want to avoid punishment, and I look for relief of *my* pain caused by *my* conscience. The Roman Catholic Church makes it easy for me to clear myself; all I have to do is sincerely regret my sins or at least seek forgiveness by a priest.

I shall not presume to declare this teaching to be false, but it only shows me a way to avoid a sentence by a judge placed outside of myself, a desire not only thoroughly selfish but also not necessarily helpful in appeasing my conscience, the merciless judge within my mind. For before I obtain forgiveness from any authority, I have to be able to forgive myself. In fact, since we have difficulty believing in some subterranean place where eternal fire is stoked by the helpers of Satan, we must assume that the pain of conscience will be the very tool used to torment the sinner. How can I escape that torment?

I can help myself only by transcending my personal limits, by realizing that I am the same as others who deserve neither punishment nor reward because, according to their innermost nature, they are striving to do the best they can, erring and stumbling on their way. Reward and punishment are only external means imposed by society to help them on their way. Only by including myself into the sinful throng, whom I forgive, can I forgive myself.

Commenting on the First Word from the cross, I observed that not judging others—accepting them—helps me to realize my unity with them and thus my unity with life in general. In discussing the last beatitude quoted, I spoke of accepting myself as a building block of life by realizing my sins and shortcomings. I have now tried to show that if acceptance of myself is to include forgiveness, it can only be by forgiving others.

Jesus illustrates that need by the parable dealing with a master who forgives a debt to his tenant until he finds out that the tenant refused to forgive his own debtor (Mt 18:23–35). On closer consideration one finds that the parable does not apply to the workings of our society. No bank will forgive my loan because I have forgiven my debtors' loans, and a thief will go to jail even though he does not mind being stolen from. Still, the parable is understandable and acceptable to everyone because it seems that a forgiving person *deserves* to be forgiven. And yet, I have tried to show no one deserves anything. On the other hand, the parable is very well suited to describing our own conscience, the judge that forgives only on condition of general forgiveness, on the very principle of not deserving anything by anyone.

This remains true whether my conscience is a God-given ability to perceive an a priori given ideal of guilt, or the concept of guilt has developed within us as a result of societal evolution.

It is worth noting that Jesus introduces the parable of the forgiving master and the ungrateful servant by likening the situation to the kingdom of heaven (Mt 18:23). We enter the kingdom of heaven—that is, we realize the divine nature uniting us—by joining others through forgiveness or rather by forgoing judgment. That is the deeper meaning of "stop judging so you may not be judged" (Mt 7:1), a meaning that does not denote a trade or reward *for* an act but rather a reward contained *in* the act. Forgiveness of our own sins is *implied* in our forgiveness of others *not granted to us in return for it.* Such is the rational basis for the experience described by Bucke in cases of sudden enlightenment that "it is not that the person escapes from sin; but he no longer sees that there is no sin in the world from which to escape,"[191] and Dostoyevsky's character's statement quoted earlier: "You do not forgive anything to anyone because there is nothing to forgive."

6

Blessed Are the Peacemakers, for They Will Be Called Children of God

Blessed Are Those Who Are Persecuted for the Sake of Righteousness, for Theirs Is the Kingdom of Heaven

The news is terrible. I remember a newspaper report in the *Los Angeles Times* about a boy who was dead with a fractured skull, fractured ribs, and BBs from a BB gun in various parts of his body, abused by his mother and her boyfriend, and unprotected by the authorities in spite of multiple reports of abuse. About the same time, a building collapsed in Bangladesh, killing several hundred textile workers in an accident caused by poor construction without regard for the safety of the proletarians who worked there. War atrocities and suicide bombings that kill innocent bystanders are reported daily.

Our first reaction is rage. Rage at the perpetrators, rage at the fates, rage at the Supreme Power allegedly ruling the world and allowing all this to happen. I discussed the wrongfulness of that reaction in the very beginning of this book. Further down in the text I suggested acceptance of life as it is where no interference is possible, but active involvement whenever there is an opportunity, acting according to the Principle of Life, our innermost nature that is identical to the essence of the universe. The realization of that nature constitutes living beyond one's mortal limits in time and space, thus becoming an active and conscious part of the kingdom of heaven, of cosmic life.

Cosmic consciousness can be approached by meditation, and in some cases it occurs as spontaneous enlightenment. But, for most of us, it is accessible only through a step-by-step process, in the form of involved participation, in living for and through others. Such involved participation is accessible to everyone, be it by word, deed, example, or even just attitude when no action is possible. I shall repeat the quote from the gospel of Matthew (Mt 25:40)—"whatever you have done for the least brothers of mine, you have done for me"—to point out that whatever we do for Jesus, who is a representative of God, we do for God and therefore for our innermost nature craving to be fulfilled.

The *doing,* whenever possible, is an essential validation of our beliefs, and this beatitude, the last to be discussed here, brings home that point. Our Self-realization requires *doing* even though it may be only in the form of nonviolent resistance.

Organized religion in general and Christian churches in particular have been performing charitable work since time immemorial. Yet during that same time the Church has been involved in persecution of heresy, in dogmatic arguments, and, worse, in subservience to ruling classes who were able to provide it with money and power.

An active struggle against poverty and exploitation of the oppressed is the center of the Liberation Theology movement,[166] and the newly elected Pope Francis I has said that addressing social problems and helping the poor and disenfranchised is more important than becoming involved in dogmatic arguments.[192] These are promising developments in an organization purported to be the bearer of Christian doctrine.

Historically, peacemakers and fighters for justice have not fared well because peace and unity demand the rejection of self-centered power, of individual, political, racial, or national supremacy. This is not acceptable to many who will not give up their sense of superiority and the material advantages usually connected with it.

Jesus, an active advocate of nonviolence, met a violent death. Three examples of peacemakers becoming victims of violence in recent times stand out. On January 30, 1948, Mahatma Gandhi was assassinated by Nathuram Godse, who thought him to be too partial to Muslims; on April 4, 1968, the white supremacist James Earl Ray killed Martin Luther King Jr., the modern exponent of nonviolent resistance to injustice; and on November 4, 1995, Yitzhak Rabin was assassinated by the religious Zionist Yigal Amir, who opposed peace with the Palestinians, especially as devised by the Oslo Accord.

The people mentioned, although for the most part not Christians, followed the Christian principle and entered heaven as I defined it above. Such a view does not deny individual survival after bodily death, but it takes away from its importance.

And now the questions arise again: What about the many saints who died simply for their beliefs? What about the female saints who died for the sole purpose of preserving their virginity? Is heaven, as we see it, closed to them? Only if they died in the egotistic belief that they are going to a paradisiacal abode where they are going to be awarded a superior position and unknown blessings—but not if they died for love of God and for dedication for the Principle of Life, for the desire to unite with God (i.e., to realize their already present identity with him). Modern man likes to see a saint stand up for social justice, clearly the challenge of Jesus. But when someone dies for his or her beliefs, the spiritual force of such an act may well have a positive effect on the plenum of Being. Thus, we must picture the death of Stephen (Acts 7:51–60), who confronts his listeners with facts unpleasant to them and is put to death for it. He says, "I see the heavens opened and the Son of Man standing at the right hand of God," and just before he dies, "Lord, do not hold this sin against them." A greater fulfillment no one can want.

SECTION 4

Thoughts on the Lord's Prayer

The "Our Father," a prayer that a Christian may utter as a sign of his or her devotion to a person who loves him or her as an affectionate parent would, can be the basis for meditation and insight even if God is not thought of as a person. It summarizes the essence of religious devotion seen as the realization of our identity with the Creative Principle and through it with all other creatures.

The prayer proceeds from addressing the One from which all Being arises, to the realization of its presence within and without. It then acquiesces to one's individual fate as part of life and part of the structure of the universe. Subsequently it reiterates our necessary relationship to the material world, then to other people, and then to the world in general, as I shall elucidate under the heading of the different devotions.

Our Father

The first word of this devotional prayer, most of the time pronounced without much attention, is of extreme importance. No individual can say that word without including other members of his or her community, perhaps all people or even all of nature. In uttering our devotion we speak with one voice arising from one common nature with the identical innermost desire for life. The devotion is addressed to the origin of life, our Father.

The address is disturbing for those who object to the male dominance in society extended to the universe. It implies a division of the creation into a male and a female principle, the former being creative and aggressive, the latter passive and receptive. This view arises from the roles played by the man and the woman in the sexual act; the man, in order to perform that act, must be aroused and aggressive, whereas the woman has only to submit without doing or even feeling anything. Obviously, such an extreme is neither common nor desirable, but it does describe the roles needed for procreation. It is consequently applied to the creative process in general, and it fits our concept of active energy and passive matter, and even the subject-predicate structure of our thoughts expressed in language.

But there is no strict division between matter and energy at the dawn of creation, and the tendency to form organized patterns is inherent in both. Sexual procreation is a relatively late development in the process of evolution. It is of great importance since it generates love, mutual dedication, and generation of new life through the merging of two beings, but it is not an original cosmic principle. The Creative Principle has no gender, whatever the grammatical one associated with it may be. Personified, it may be addressed as Father or as Mother, depending on whether we want to emphasize its aggressive or nurturing aspect, since we are unable to visualize a person who is not endowed with gender. The God of the Hebrews, at least when addressed as Lord (Adonai), is male, and is also referred to as "He" in the Bible. Thus Jesus using the language and the concepts of his time refers to God as Father.

Primitive cultures, aware of the creatively nurturing aspect of the earth, divinized it as mother so that "for the first 200,000 years of human life on earth God was female."[193] Vanamali, in the book *Shakti, Realm of the Divine Mother*, writes, "Indian pictorial representations of God in ancient times took both male and female forms. Over time, the universal form of the motionless absolute came to be associated with the male form and the manifested energy of nature with the female form … In the words of Vishnu in the Skanda Puruna: 'the male and female are eternal principles involved in the projection of the universe … Fundamentally they are one, as gold and ornaments made of it are one.' This two in one existence became known as Purusha and Prakriti or Shiva and Shakti."[194] Here then the male and female principles are presented as having equal importance, inseparably bound together.

Jesus says, according to the Gospel of John (Jn 4:24), that God is Spirit, and in his first letter, John says that God is love (1 Jn 4:8). The Hebrew word for *spirit* is *Ruah*, which is feminine, as it is in

Aramaic, the language of Jesus. It is neuter in Greek and masculine in Latin. The gender of love also depends on the language spoken. Thus, neither spirit nor love has a gender associated with it except as a matter of grammar.

Based on the foregoing considerations, we are probably entitled to say that if people wish to pray to Our Mother instead of Our Father, they would not commit a theological error, although it would have a disturbing effect on the traditional sound of the prayer, yet no one should dare to substitute *my* for *our*.

Who Art in Heaven

Here again the address contains a small word of paramount importance. By saying *who art,* we affirm the existence of God. Such existence is self-evident if we remove from our concept of God all that has to do with the projection of qualities of a terrestrial judge or potentate. I am not maintaining that such a projection is necessarily mistaken; I am only saying that the existence of a divine potentate cannot be proved and has to be accepted on faith, whereas the Principle of Existence, a Creative Principle with which we can identify, is self-evident.

The name of God, the only one, according to biblical wisdom, pronounced by himself, is "I AM" (Ex 3:14), so in saying, "Our Father who art," we are addressing God by his self-proclaimed name, one that represents him as the essence of Being.

The expression *in heaven* may seem like a remnant from times when heaven was thought to be a dome above the earth, supporting several layers of paradisiacal dwellings, the uppermost inhabited by God. People could still believe in such a heavenly abode when they could no longer accept some high mountain, such as Olympus, to be God's dwelling place. But now, since we know that heaven is not a firmament but rather a boundless space appearing blue because of the diffusion of light, it fits much better our concept of God as a creative essence immanent in the cosmos with all its infinite variety of the immense and the infinitesimal.

"God is in heaven" means that God permeates the entire cosmos and, by the realization that we belong to that vast system as a conscious part thereof, we attain Cosmic Consciousness and transcend our mortal limits, an attainment I have equated with entering the kingdom of heaven.

Hallowed Be Thy Name

The name of a person or a thing is the immediate transfer of a concept into the tools of language; it evokes the concept as soon as it is perceived. It may well be that "a rose by any other name would smell as sweet," but we would have to become first used to the new name to associate it with the same fragrance and the same loveliness. God's name may evoke widely differing concepts, but ultimately it will always be that of an entity superior to everything else. But the concept that is superior to everything by comprising everything is that of Being in its manifold manifestations. Therefore we have to fall back on the concept of God as the creator and maintainer of the world, be it as a conscious person or a principle.

This is confirmed by God's self-given name "I AM" and by our address "who art," as I have discussed. It indicates that we honor the name of God not as we would honor that of another person, no matter how dear or how socially elevated, but as the ground of all Being, including our own, thus exceeding everything else in importance, uniting us with everything else, and permitting us to live therein.

Thy Kingdom Come

The kingdom of God must be the same as the kingdom of heaven, for according to the second devotion of this prayer, heaven is the abode of God. We have concluded as discussed under the heading of the first beatitude, and as is clearly said by the gospel of Thomas, that that abode "is inside you and it is outside you"[153] and that we share this abode with God knowingly when we realize our identity with him (i.e., obtain Cosmic Consciousness through Self-realization). That is the coming of the kingdom.

Nevertheless, nothing I said contradicts our hope that an ideal state of our world community, a terrestrial kingdom of God, might someday be established. That must be our goal. For, as I discussed previously, the realization of the kingdom of heaven within us requires a sincere effort to improve the conditions in our environment. On the other hand, such an effort is not possible unless it is rooted within us.

Thy Will Be Done on Earth as It Is in Heaven

If God micromanages the world and with it my life, then anything that happens to me is to my ultimate advantage and I happily conform to that will.

But if, as I suggested earlier, God has partially withdrawn from the world to allow pain and sin to exist in order to define goodness, and if these evils are spread out arbitrarily as from Pandora's box, forever challenging me, then the will of God is that I lead a full life, seeking the good and being a building stone in cosmic life. In Seneca's Letter XCVI, already mentioned under the heading of "blessed are those who mourn," the writer says, "I follow Him because my soul wills it, not because I must."[105]

Heaven, in our terms, denotes the abode of God that is within and without me. It is therefore the entire cosmos wherein God dwells, forever seeking a "creative advance into novelty." That advance is God's will as well as mine, and it concerns the entire cosmic mechanism above and below, expressed in biblical terms "in heaven and on earth."

6

Give Us This Day Our Daily Bread

Regarding this devotion, Martin Luther says, "God gives their daily bread to all kinds of wicked people. We ask in this prayer for the realization that it comes from Him, and that we may be grateful for it."[195] He then proceeds by saying that "our daily bread" is the entire environment that nourishes and maintains us. If we substitute *Creative Principle* for *God*, then even the atheist should be able to utter this devotion as interpreted by Luther with conviction and sincerity.

The material environment that gave rise to me and that keeps me alive is not shaped by a wicked demiurge; it is a manifestation of an all-pervading Creative Principle that is my innermost essence as well.

I am not imprisoned in this world as some devout individuals may think, receiving my daily bread so I can stay here until I am liberated; I live through this world and for this world as an integral part of it. This devotion then expresses my positive relationship with the material world surrounding me, again seen as a manifestation of the will of God.

And Forgive Us Our Trespasses as We Forgive Those Who Trespass against Us

If there is an a priori ideal of justice and of deserved punishment, then we might deserve forgiveness and mercy if we exercise it ourselves. But throughout this book, I have maintained that, according to our innermost nature, we all strive to accomplish the good, erring and stumbling on our way. If that is the case, then the only way to soothe my conscience, conditioned by millenniums of belief in retributive justice, is to deny the guilt of others, including myself in their erring throng; in other words, I need to forgive anyone anything he or she may have wrought against me or against others.

8

And Lead Us Not into Temptation but Deliver Us from Evil

The text in the New Jerusalem Bible says, "And do not put us to the test," which can mean the same as "lead us not into temptation," whereas the New American Bible prefers, "And do not subject us to the final test," referring to a severe trial before the end of the age predicted by Jewish apocalyptic writings. Thus the translators express some doubt whether current or final temptations are meant. However, the petition *but deliver us from Evil* or *the Evil One* clearly indicates a desire to be rid of Satan always lurking around the corner or, in more worldly terms, of misguided incitements of the ego and the id as well as of faulty reasoning—a plea to forgo temptation.

A temptation is anything distracting us from fulfillment of our innermost nature, namely participating in the creative advance into novelty and realizing our unity with the advance of cosmos as a whole. As such this devotion relates not only to our relations with other humans but with our entire environment as well.

Most temptations and transgressions are related to our "original sin," our unavoidable opposition to other beings by virtue of our existence as individuals. We sin any time we exaggerate the adversarial aspect of this relationship, and we are blessed any time we are able to overcome it, at least in part. The adversarial aspect comes to the fore any time we consider other individuals as well as things in our environment as objects rather than fellow subjects. It is the id and the ego that try to objectify everything and everybody they come in contact with for the purpose of separate, individual survival. Murder and theft are examples of such behavior, but using friendship for ulterior motives or treating one's sexual partner purely as an object of control and physical satisfaction fall into the same category.

The temptations encountered by Jesus according to Matthew 4:1–11 go deeper and are representative of three essential impediments to our Self-realization, a precondition for Cosmic Consciousness.

"Command that these stones become loaves of bread," or in other words, "Use your power to make nature a source of material well-being" is a view characteristic of materialism and the utilitarian philosophy of those who cannot see beyond man's material needs. It is, of course, also a challenge to tempt God, but Jesus's response, "one does not live by bread alone," supports the first interpretation of that temptation. Material well-being is not to be despised as incompatible with spiritual accomplishment, but it must not obscure our ultimate purpose in life, namely living for and through others and thus achieving unity with the entire creation and through it with God, the Creative Principle of Life indwelling in matter.

The next temptation concerns the essence of religiousness, the finding of the Creative Principle within ourselves, something that cannot be realized if we look for external proofs for the existence of God, if we "tempt God" by asking him to prove himself.

Miracles and answered prayers prove nothing because they can always be explained away by coincidence or mass hypnosis, or their veracity can simply be doubted. A conscious Being transcending space and time can never be proved to exist since I cannot even prove that the person nearest to me is not acting as an automaton. How can I then prove some sort of conscious management of the world? Josh McDowell wrote a book attempting to substantiate the historical data of the New Testament.[196] It is certainly a worthwhile effort and interesting reading, but the essence of religion lies in the recognition of the Principle of Life of which we are part and not in the historical veracity of the Scriptures .

It is only within myself that I can experience the divine Principle of Life that unites me to the entire cosmos. The kingdom of heaven is truly within me. The ability to experience such a unity we have referred to as "Cosmic Consciousness" through "Self-realization." Any attempt to "prove" the existence of God as an outside agency must fail and open the door to atheism.

Both the first and the second temptation have to do with materialism: first the obsession with material goods and second the obsession with material facts.

The final temptation reaches beyond that. It has to do with the will to live but a thwarted will, limited to one's own id, modified by a pragmatic ego. Because it is partially rooted in our innermost nature, it is extremely strong, but the only relation with others and with our entire environment it achieves is making objects out of them. The temptation is to expand one's life—one's being—through power. It is a misguided notion, for if we live *through* others but not *for* others, we include them in our existence but do not give of ourselves to them. Thus, we live only for ourselves and our world dies with us. Feuerbach refers to it as "the desire to devour the object instead of the desire to let oneself be consumed and devoured by the object."[197]

It is worth noting that many sins emphasized by organized religion, such as missing mass, sexual intercourse unsanctioned by ritual, not being baptized, not confessing one's sins, neglecting to fast—in short, obligations installed mostly by tradition—are not derivable from the definition of sin presented above. These obligations establish our relationship with the Church and thus indirectly serve our closeness to God. They are worth being complied with whenever possible. But they become worthless if we, while obeying them, fall prey to the temptations reported above.

9

For Thine Is the Kingdom and the Power and the Glory for Ever and Ever, Amen

The doxology at the end of the Lord's Prayer, found in many manuscripts as well as many translations of the New Testament, is omitted in the New American Bible as well as in the New Jerusalem Bible. It is included in the German translation of Martin Luther. According to *A New Catholic Commentary on the Holy Scripture,* it "probably crept in from liturgical usage."[198] We find it attached to the Lord's Prayer in as ancient a document as the Didache without mention of the kingdom.[199]

If we not only believe in a personal God but also project onto him the attributes of a terrestrial ruler, the doxology has a definite meaning, and it may well have been composed with such an idea in mind. But even if that is the case, we may read into it a summation of what I tried to show in this brief work: Jesus's life and death showing a way to Self-realization and Cosmic Consciousness.

God's kingdom "does not belong to this world" (Jn 18:36) if the latter term is meant to designate an organized society headed by a ruler. It is not a state certain to exist in the future but rather "the collective power of good," which is our innermost nature as well as the sum of forces accomplishing "a creative advance into novelty." In that kingdom, realized by searching within us and acting accordingly, we abide united.

The power of God is not a power exercised against anyone's will but rather the power to provide us with our ultimate good, the fulfillment of our innermost nature, and, with it, life beyond ourselves.

The glory of God is not the glory possessed by someone by virtue of being placed very high above us but rather the triumph of our innermost nature, realized from within. No greater glory is achievable, for there is no higher good.

The words *forever and ever* denote not an endless duration in time but a transcending of our individual temporal limits through unity with God.

BIBLIOGRAPHY

http://www.animal-symbols.com/snake-symbol.html.

"Catholic Encyclopedia." http://www.newadvent.org/cathen/15764c.htm.

"Liturgy of the Hours." http://www.ebreviary.com.

"The Mind of Mahatma Gandhi." http://www.mkgandhi.org/momgandhi/chap18.htm.

"Sabra and Shatilla." http://jewishvoiceforpeace.org/content/sabra-and-shatilla.

The Hindu Tradition. New York: The Modern Library, 1966.

A New Catholic Commentary on the Holy Scripture. Nashville, TN: Thomas Nelson, 1969.

Encyclopaedia Britannica. Chicago: William Benton, 1972.

The Cambridge Dictionary of Philosophy. Audi, Robert, ed. Cambridge, England, 1996.

The Columbia History of Western Philosophy. New York: Columbia University Press, 1999.

The Didache: Text, Translation, Analysis and Commentary. Collegeville, MN: Liturgical Press, 2003.

The Thirteen Principal Upanishads, 2nd ed. Translated by Robert Ernest Hume. Oxford, England: Oxford University Press, 2003.

The Complete Dictionary of Symbols. San Francisco: Chronicle Books, 2005.

Alt, Franz. *Frieden Ist Moeglich. Die Politik Der Bergpredigt.* Muenchen Zurich: R. Piper. Verlag, 1983.

Aslan, Reza. *Zealot.* New York: Random House, 2013.

Attar. "Rabi'a: Her Words and Life in 'Memorial of the Friends of God.'" In *Early Islamic Mysticism*, edited by Michael A. Sells, 151. New York: Paulist Press, 1996.

Bailey, Alice A. *Consciousness of the Atom.* San Bernardino, CA: Create Space Independent Publishing Platform, 2013.

Bentham, Jeremy. *Theory of Legislation.* Translated from the French of Etienne Dumont by R. Hildreth. Vol. 1. Boston: Weeks, Jordan, 1840.

———. *The Principles of Morals and Legislation.* Amherst, NY: Prometheus Books, 1988.

Berdyaev, Nicolai. *Dukh I Real'nost' (Spirit and Reality).* Moscow: Astrel, 2011.

Bergen, Helen. "Living One's Truth" http://www.vatican.va/roman curia/pontifical councils/interelg/documents/rc pc interelg doc 20030203 new-age en.htlm.

Bergson, Henry. *Creative Evolution.* Translated by Arthur Mitchell. New York: Modern Library, 1944.

Boehme, Jacob. *Werke.* Vol. 33. Frankfurt am Main: Deutscher Klassiker Verlag im Taschenbuch, 2009.

Bracken, Joseph A., SJ. *The One and the Many.* Grand Rapids, MI: William B. Eerdmans, 2001.

———. *Christianity and Process Thought.* Philadelphia: Templeton Foundation, 2006.

Bradley, H. *Ethical Studies.* New York: Cambridge University Press, 2012.

Brandon, S. G. F. "The Death of James the Just, a New Interpretation." In *Studies in Mysticism and Religion*. Jerusalem: Magnus Press, 1967.

Buber, Martin. *Ich Und Du.* Heidelberg, Germany: Verlag Lambert Schneider, 1983.

Bucke, Richard Maurice, MD. *Cosmic Consciousness.* New Hyde Park, NY: University Books, 1961.

Bultmann, Rudolf. *Theology of the New Testament.* Translated by Kendrick Grobel. Vol. 1. Waco, TX: Baylor University Press, 2007.

Burke, Edmond. *Reflections on the French Revolution.* Cambridge, England: Cambridge University Press, 1929.

Churchill, Ward. *A Little Matter of Genocide.* San Francisco: City Lights Books, 1997.

Cobb Jr., John B. *Christ in a Pluralistic Age.* Eugene, OR: Wipf and Stock, 1998.

Cohen, Abraham. *Everyone's Talmud.* New York: Schocken Books, 1949.

Copleston, Frederick. *Religion and the One.* New York: Crossroad, 1980.

Curtis, Anthony. "Introduction." In *The Razor's Edge by Somerset Maugham.* New York: Penguin Books, 1992.

Dayal, Har, MA, PhD. *The Bodhisattva Doctrine in Buddhist Sanskrit Literature.* Delhi: Motilal Banarsidass, 1999.

de Quervain, DJ, et al. "The Neural Basis for Altruistic Punishment." *Science* 305, August 27, 2004.

Deutsch, Eliot. *Advaita Vedanda.* Honolulu: University of Hawaii Press, 1969.

Dostoyevsky, Fyodor. *Letters of Fyodor Michailovitch Dostoevsky to Family and Friends.* Translated by Ethel Golburn Mayne, 1914. *Quotes.* Found on http://en.wikiquote.org/wiki/Fyodor_Dostoyevsky.

Dostoyevsky, Fyodor. *Becy (Demons)* In *Collected Works* Volume 7. Gosudarstvennoye Izdatel'stvo Khudozhestvennoy Literatury, Moscow, 1957.

Dubos, Rene. *A God Within*. New York: Charles Scribner's Sons, 1972.

Eckhart, Meister. *Deutsche Predigten Und Traktate*. Translated into modern German from Middle High German by Joseph Quint. Zurich: Diogenes Verlag A.G., 1979.

Edwards, Denis. *Jesus the Wisdom of God*. Maryknoll, NY: Orbis Books, 1995.

Einstein, Albert. *Ideas and Opinions*. New York: Crown, 1982.

Ellis, Havelock. *The New Spirit*. New York: Boni and Liveright, Publishers, 1921.

Feuerbach, Ludwig. *The Essence of Christianity*. New York: Harper & Row, 1957.

Feuerbach, Ludwig. *Thoughts on Death and Immortality*. Translated by James A. Massey. Berkeley: University of California Press, 1980.

Fox, Matthew. *Breakthrough, Meister Eckharts Creation Spirituality in New Translation*. Garden City, NY: Image Books, 1980.

Fox, Matthew. *The Coming of the Cosmic Christ*. San Francisco: Harper, 1988.

Fox, Matthew. *Original Blessing*. New York: Jeremy P. Thatcher/ Putnam, 2000.

Frankl, Viktor E., MD, PhD. *Man's Search for Ultimate Meaning*. New York: Basic Books, 2000.

Funk, Robert W. *The Five Gospels. What Did Jesus Really Say?* New York: Harper One, 1997.

———. *The Five Gospels. What Did Jesus Really Say?* New York: Harper One, 1997.

Garvey, Stephen P. *Beyond Repair? America's Death Penalty*. Durham, NC: Duke University Press, 2003.

Gaster, Theodor Herzl. *Passover, Its History and Traditions*. New York: Henry Schuman, 1949.

Graves, Kersey. *The World's Sixteen Crucified Saviors or Christianity before Christ*. Kila, MT: Kessinger Publishing Company, originally published in 1875, year of cited reprint not given.

Gray, Donald P. *The One and the Many*. New York: Herder and Herder, 1969.

Gutierrez, Gustavo. *A Theology of Liberation*. Translated by Sister Caridad Inda and John Eagleson. Maryknoll, NY: Orbis Books, 1988.

Haight, Roger, SJ. *Jesus Symbol of God*. Maryknoll, NY: Orbis Books, 1999.

Haldane, J. B. S., FRS. *The Inequality of Man*. Harmondsworth Middlesex England: Penguin Books, 1937.

Hamer, Dean. *The God Gene*. New York: Anchor Books, 2005.

Hawking, Stephen, and Leonard Mlodinow. *The Grand Design*. New York: Bantam Books, 2010.

Hitchens, Christopher. *god is not Great: How Religion Spoils Everything*. New York: Twelve, 2007.

Hsi, Chu. *Learning to Be a Sage*. Translated by Daniel K. Gardner. Berkeley: University of California Press, 1990.

J.H. Personal communication, 2014.

James, William. *Varieties of Religious Experience*. Charleston, SC: Bibliobazaar.

John Paul I. http://www.ewtn.com/library/papaldoc/jp2tb26.htm.

John-Julian, Fr., OJN. *The Complete Julian of Norwich*. Brewster, MA: Paraclete, 2009.

Josephus. "The Antiquities of the Jews." In *The Works of Josephus*. Peabody, MA: Hendrickson, 1987.

Kington, Tom, and Henry Chu. "Pope Seeks to Shift Catholic Church's Priority from Dogma to Mercy." *Los Angeles Times*, September 19, 2013.

Laufer, Nathaniel. *Leading the Passover Journey.* Woodstock, VT: Jewish Lights, 2005.

Leloup, Jean-Yves. *The Gospel of Mary Magdalene.* Translated by Joseph Rowe. Rochester, VT: Inner Traditions, 2002.

————. *The Gospel of Philip.* Translated by Joseph Rowe from the French. Rochester, VT: Inner Traditions, 2004.

————. *The Gospel of Thomas.* Translated by Joseph Rowe. Rochester, VT: Inner Traditions, 2005.

Linssen, Robert. *Living Zen.* New York: Grove Weidenfeld, 1958.

Long, Jeffrey D. "A Whiteheadian Vedanta." In *Handbook of Process Theology,* edited by Jay McDaniel and Donna Bowman, 273. St. Louis, MO, 2006.

Luther, Dr. Martin. *Der Kleine Katechismus.* Fechenheim, Germany: Allg. Pfarrwitwenkasse als Verlegerin bei Maindruck, 1946.

Mahesh Yogi, Maharishi. *Science of Being and Art of Living.* New York: Penguin, 2001.

Maier, Johann. *Die Kabbalah.* Muenchen: Verlag C. H. Beck, 1995.

Mattox, John Mark. *Saint Augustine and the Theory of War.* New York: Continuum, 2006.

Maugham, W. Somerset. *The Razor's Edge,* New York: Penguin Books, 1992.

McDowell, Josh. *New Evidence That Demands a Verdict.* Nashville, TN: Thomas Nelson, 1999.

McGiffert, Arthur Cushman. *The Apostles' Creed.* New York: Charles Scribner's Sons, 1902.

Moltmann, Jürgen. *The Way of Jesus Christ.* Translated by Margaret Kohl. Minneapolis, MN: Fortress, 1933.

Nelstrop, Louise. *Christian Mysticism.* Burlington, VT: Ashgate, 2009.

Noss, John B. *Man's Religions,* 6th ed. New York: Macmillan and Collier McMillan, 1980.

Ortega y Gasset, Jose. *Meditaciones De Quijote*. Madrid, Spain: Catedra, Letras Hispanicas, 2012.

Paine, Thomas. *Rights of Man*. Mineola, New York: Dover, 1999.

Parmenides, "Poem Stanza Viii," philoctetes.free.fr/parmenides unicode.htm. Copyright Samuel Bereau (2014).

Pearce, Matt, and Molly Hennessy-Fiske. "'American Sniper' Killed at Gun Range," *Los Angeles Times*, February 4, 2013.

Pope, Stephen J. *The Evolution of Altruism and the Ordering of Love*. Washington, DC: Georgetown University Press, 2007.

Post, Stephen G. *Unlimited Love. Altruism, Compassion and Service*. Philadelphia: Templeton Foundation, 2003.

Randall, Francis B. "Introduction. Marx the Romantic." In *The Communist Manifesto by Karl Marx and Friedrich Engels*, edited by Joseph Katz. New York: Pocket Books, 1964.

Ratzinger, Joseph Cardinal. *Introduction to Christianity*. San Francisco, CA: Ignatius Press, 1990.

Rich, Josiah D., MD, MPH, Sarah E. Wakeman, MD, and Samuel L. Dickman, AB. "Medicine and the Epidemic of Incarceration in the United States." *New England Journal of Medicine*, June 2, 2011.

Riley-Smith, Jonathan. *The Crusades*. New York: Continuum, 2005.

Rosenthal, Norman E., MD. *Transcendence. Healing and Transformation Through Transcendental Meditation*. New York: Jeremy P. Tarcher/Penguin, 2012.

Ross, Jennifer, "Torah Class" http://www.torahclass.com/archived-articles/429-anav-by-jennifer-ross.

Russell, Bertrand. *A History of Western Philosophy*. New York: Simon and Schuster, 1972.

Schleiermacher, Friedrich. *Ueber Die Religion*. Stuttgart: Philipp Reclam jun., 2010, first printing 1799.

Scholem, Gershom G. *Major Trends in Jewish Mysticism*. New York: Schocken Books, 1974.

Schweitzer, Albert. *The Teaching of Reverence for Life*. Translated by Richard and Clara Winston from German. New York: Holt, Rinehart and Winston, 1965.

Sellars, John. *Stoicism*. Berkeley: University of California Press, 2006.

Seneca, "Moral Letters to Lucilius/Letter 96." http://en.wikisource. org/wiki/Moral_letters_to_Lucilius/Letter_96.

Shakespeare, William. *Hamlet* in *The Annotated Shakespeare*. Editor A. L. Rowse, Volume III. New York: Clarkson N. Potter Inc., 1978

Sheen, Fulton J. *The Seven Last Words*. New York: Society of St. Paul, 1996.

Sheldrake, Rupert, Terence McKenna, and Ralph Abraham. *Chaos, Creativity and Cosmic Consciousness,* Rochester, VT: Park Street Press, 2001.

Sjöö, Monica, and Barbara Mor. *The Great Cosmic Mother*. New York: Harper One, 1991.

Skinner, B.F. *About Behaviorism*. New York: Vintage Books, 1976.

Steinberg, David. "Where Is Your Heart? Some Body Part Metaphors and Euphemisms in Biblical Hebrew." http://www.adath-shalom.ca/body-_metaphors_bib_hebrew.htm.

Teihard de Chardin, Pierre. *Le Phénomène Humain*. Paris: Editions du Seuil, 1955.

Teilhard de Chardin, Pierre. *Le Milieu Divin*. Paris: Editions du Seuil, 1957.

Teilhard de Chardin, Pierre. *The Phenomenon of Man*. Translated by Bernard Wall. New York: Harper Perennial Modern Thought, 2008.

Tillich, Paul. *Systematic Theology*. Vol. I. Chicago: University of Chicago Press, 1971.

———. *Systematic Theology.* Vol. II. Chicago: University of Chicago Press, 1971.

———. *Systematische Theologie.* Vol. II. Berlin: de Gruyter, 1987.

Tolstoy, Leo. *Collected Works (Russian Edition).* Vol. 12. Moscow: Khudozhestvennaya Literatura, 1964.

———. *The Kingdom of God Is Within You.* Translated by Constance Garnett: Wildside, 2006.

Tsu, Lao. *Tao Te Ching.* Translated by D. C. Lau. London: Penguin Books, 1963.

Vanamali. *Shakti: Realm of the Divine Mother.* Rochester, VT: Inner Traditions, 2008.

Weinberg, Stephen. *The First Three Minutes,* cited by Edwards, p. 6.

Weiss, Kenneth. "Runaway Population Growth Often Fuels Youth Driven Uprisings." *Los Angeles Times,* July 22, 2012.

Whitehead, Alfred North. *Process and Reality.* New York: The Free Press, 1985.

Yancey, Philip. *Where Is God When It Hurts?* Grand Rapids, MI: Zondervan, 1977.

Yogananda, Paramahansa. *Journey to Self-Realization.* Vol. III. Los Angeles: Self-Realization Fellowship, 2000.

REFERENCES AND COMMENTS

The biblical quotes are taken from the New American Bible, 1987 edition.

The text of the Lord's Prayer is that recited during the Roman Catholic Mass.

The quotes from the New Jerusalem Bible refer to the "Saints' Devotional Edition" 2002.

Unless otherwise noted, the translations from the quoted texts are by the author.

ENDNOTES

1   Richard Maurice Bucke, MD, *Cosmic Consciousness* (New Hyde Park, NY: University Books, 1961), 277.

2   Matthew Fox, *The Coming of the Cosmic Christ* (San Francisco: Harper, 1988), 7.

3   Ibid., 133.

4   Jürgen Moltmann, *The Way of Jesus Christ*, trans. Margaret Kohl (Minneapolis, MN: Fortress Press, 1933), 276.

5   Ibid., 277.

6   Denis Edwards, *Jesus the Wisdom of God* (Maryknoll, NY: Orbis Books, 1995), 166.

7   Roger Haight, SJ, *Jesus Symbol of God* (Maryknoll, NY Orbis Books, 1999), 333.

8   Joseph A. Bracken, SJ, *Christianity and Process Thought* (Philadelphia: Templeton Foundation, 2006), 96 ff.

9   Havelock Ellis, *The New Spirit*, p. 232, cited by William James in *Varieties of Religious Experience* (Charleston, SC: Bibliobazaar, 2007), 57.

10 Christopher Hitchens, *god is not Great: How Religion Spoils Everything* (New York: Twelve, 2007), 12.

11 Alfred North Whitehead, *Process and Reality,* corrected edition (New York: Free Press, 1985), 348 ff. Whitehead and the Process Theologians who followed him do not limit the concept of God

to the stated principle, but it is of a foremost significance in their view.

[12] Albert Schweitzer, *The Teaching of Reverence for Life*, trans. Richard and Clara Winston (from German). (New York: Holt, Rinehart and Winston, 1965), 26.

[13] Henry Bergson, *Creative Evolution*, trans. Arthur Mitchell (New York: Modern Library, 1944).

[14] Sheldrake, McKenna, and Abraham, *Chaos, Creativity and Cosmic Consciousness* (Rochester, VT: Park Street Press, 2001), 172.

[15] Stephen Hawking and Leonard Mlodinow, *The Grand Design* (New York: Bantam Books, 2010), 135.

[16] Rene Dubos, *A God Within* (New York: Charles Scribner's Sons, 1972), 28.

[17] Alice A. Bailey, *Consciousness of the Atom* (San Bernardino, CA: Create Space Independent Publishing Platform, 2013), 9.

[18] Ibid., 24.

[19] *The Cambridge Dictionary of Philosophy*, Robert Audi, general Editor. (Cambridge, England: 1996), 352.

[20] Alfred North Whitehead, *Process and Reality* (New York: The Free Press, 1985), 22.

[21] Stephen Weinberg, *The First Three Minutes*, cited by Edwards, 6, 144.

[22] Pierre Teilhard de Chardin, *The Phenomenon of Man*, trans. Bernard Wall (New York: Harper Perennial Modern Thought, 2008), 232.

[23] Eliot Deutsch, *Advaita Vedanda* (Honolulu: University of Hawaii Press, 1969), 48–49.

[24] Ibid., 14.

[25] Alfred North Whitehead, *Process and Reality* (New York: The Free Press, 1985), 343.

[26] Ibid., 345.

27 *The Thirteen Principal Upanishads*, 2nd ed., trans. Robert Ernest Hume. (Oxford, England: Oxford University Press, 2003), 246 ff.

28 Ludwig Feuerbach, *Thoughts on Death and Immortality*, trans. James A. Massey (Berkeley: University of California Press, 1980), 114.

29 Ibid., 173.

30 Friedrich Schleiermacher, *Ueber Die Religion* (Stuttgart: Philipp Reclam jun., 2010), 87 ff.

31 Paramahansa Yogananda, *Journey to Self-Realization*, Vol. III (Los Angeles: Self-Realization Fellowship, 2000), 435.

32 Parmenides, "Poem Stanza Viii," philoctetes.free.fr/parmenidesunicode.htm. Copyright Samuel Bereau (2014). Translated by John Burnet, 1892.

33 *The Columbia History of Western Philosophy*, Richard H. Popkin, editor (New York: Columbia University Press, 1999), 108 ff.

34 Meister Eckhart, *Deutsche Predigten Und Traktate*, translated into modern German from Middle High German by Joseph Quint (Zurich: Diogenes Verlag A.G., 1979), 273. Predigt 26. Noli timere eos, qui corpus …

35 Lao Tsu, *Tao Te Ching*, trans. D. C. Lau (London: Penguin Books, 1963); Eckhart.

36 Frederick Copleston, *Religion and the One* (New York: Crossroad, 1980).

37 Joseph A. Bracken, SJ, *The One and the Many* (Grand Rapids, MI: William B. Eerdmans, 2001).

38 Donald P. Gray, *The One and the Many* (New York: Herder and Herder, 1969).

39 Louise Nelstrop, *Christian Mysticism* (Burlington, VT: Ashgate, 2009). Coauthored by Kevin Magill and Bradley B. Onishi.

40 William James, *Varieties of Religious Experience* (Charleston, SC: Bibliobazaar, 2007).

41 Richard Maurice Bucke, MD, *Cosmic Consciousness* (New Hyde Park, NY: University Books, 1961) 7 ff.

42 Pierre Teihard de Chardin, *Le Phénomène Humain* (Paris: Editions du Seuil, 1955), 30.

43 Jeffrey D. Long, "A Whiteheadian Vedanta," in *Handbook of Process Theology*, ed. Jay McDaniel and Donna Bowman (St. Louis, MO: Chalice Press, 2006), 273.

44 Robert Linssen, *Living Zen* (New York: Grove Weidenfeld, 1958), 152. This citation is not an attempt to reconcile Buddhism and Christianity and their different approaches to life. It is only meant to show that some final conclusions cannot be avoided, no matter where one starts out.

45 Paul Tillich, *Systematic Theology*, Vol. II (Chicago: University of Chicago Press, 1971), 70.

46 Paul Tillich, *Systematische Theologie*, Vol. II (Berlin: de Gruyter, 1987), 80.

47 Maharishi Mahesh Yogi, *Science of Being and Art of Living* (New York: Penguin Group, A Plume Book, 2001), 27 ff.

48 Ibid., 175 ff.

49 Norman E. Rosenthal, MD, *Transcendence. Healing and Transformation Through Transcendental Meditation* (New York: Jeremy P. Tarcher/Penguin, 2012).

50 Rudolf Bultmann, *Theology of the New Testament*, trans. Kendrick Grobel, Vol. 1 (Waco, TX: Baylor University Press, 2007), 259.

51 Meister Eckhart *Deutsche Predigten und Traktate*. Translated into modern German from Middle High German by Joseph Quint (Zurich: Diogenes Verlag A.G., 1979), 186. Predigt 7 "Justi vivent in eternam."

52 Paul Tillich, *Systematic Theology*, Vol. I (Chicago: University of Chicago Press, 1971), 85.

53 Rudolf Bultmann, *Theology of the New Testament*. Translated by Kendrick Grobel. (Waco,TX: Baylor University Press, 2007. Vol. 1,12.

54 H. Bradley, *Ethical Studies* (New York: Cambridge University Press, 2012), 271. Originally published in 1876. I did not capitalize the word *self* in keeping with the original, but undoubtedly the Self is meant.

55 Viktor E. Frankl, MD, PhD, *Man's Search for Ultimate Meaning* (New York: Basic Books, 2000), 84. Here I took the liberty of capitalizing *Self* even though the author did not.

56 Har Dayal, MA, PhD, *The Bodhisattva Doctrine in Buddhist Sanskrit Literature* (Delhi: Motilal Banarsidass, 1999), 4. See my comment under reference 44.

57 Stephen J. Pope, *The Evolution of Altruism and the Ordering of Love* (Washington, DC: Georgetown University Press, 2007).

58 Stephen G. Post, *Unlimited Love. Altruism, Compassion and Service* (Philadelphia and London: Templeton Foundation, 2003).

59 Paul Tillich, *Systematic Theology*, (Chicago: Chicago University Press, 1971). Volume 2, 70.

60 Chu Hsi, *Learning to Be a Sage* (Berkeley: University of California Press, 1990), 90. Translation and commentary by Daniel K. Gardner.

61 B. F. Skinner, *About Behaviorism* (New York: Vintage Books, 1976), 211.

62 Albert Einstein, *Ideas and Opinions* (New York: Crown, 1982), cited by Matthew Fox, 161.

63 Jean-Yves Leloup, *The Gospel of Mary Magdalene*, trans. Joseph Rowe (Rochester, VT: Inner Traditions, 2002), 31. Translation from the Coptic and commentary by Jean-Yves Leloup.

64 Abraham Cohen, *Everyone's Talmud* (New York: Schocken Books, 1949), 77.

65 Gershom G. Scholem, *Major Trends in Jewish Mysticism* (New York: Schocken Books, 1974), 241.

66 Johann Maier, *Die Kabbalah* (Muenchen: Verlag C. H. Beck, 1995), 166.

67 Chu His *Learning to be a Sage*, trans. Daniel K. Gardner (Berkeley: University of California Press, 1990), 145.

68 Jean-Ives Leloup, *The Gospel of Mary Magdalene,* 33, 35. Ignorance as a cause of sin is a concept found in the teachings of Gnosticism, but in quoting it I do not subscribe to the basic idea of Gnosticism that the material world is evil, nor do I believe that the common tendency to call many of the apocryphal Gospels "Gnostic" is justified. See *The Cambridge Dictionary of Philosophy*, p. 298, for the usual definition of Gnosticism.

69 Gershom G. Scholem, *Major Trends in Jewish Mysticism* (New York: Schocken Books, 1974), 260 ff.

70 Jacob Boehme, *Werke*, vol. 33 (Frankfurt am Main: Deutscher Klassiker Verlag im Taschenbuch, 2009), 55. Originally printed in Amsterdam, 1656.

71 Lao Tzu, *Tao Te Ching*, trans. D. C. Lau (London: Penguin Group, 1963). Commentary by the translator, 125.

72 Bertrand Russell, *A History of Western Philosophy* (New York: Simon and Schuster, 1972), 257.

73 Richard Maurice Bucke, MD, *Cosmic Consciousness* (New Hyde Park, NY: University Books, 1961), 61.

74 J. H. Personal communication, 2014.

75 Dean Hamer, *The God Gene* (New York: Anchor Books, 2005), 143.

76 Meister Eckhart, *Deutsche Predigten und Traktate.* Translated into modern German from Middle High German by Joseph Quint (Zurich: Diogenes Verlag A.G., 1979), Predigt 32, "Beati pauperes spiritu …" p.305.

77 Fyodor Dostoyevsky, *Letters of Fyodor Michailovitch Dostoevsky to Family and Friends*, trans. Ethel Golburn Mayne (1914), Letter XXI to Mme. Fonvisin (1854), 71. Found on http://en.wikiquote.org/wiki/Fyodor_Dostoevsky.

78 Robert W. Funk, *The Five Gospels: What Did Jesus Really Say?* (New York: Harper One, 1997). Coauthored by Roy W. Hoover and the Jesus Seminar.

79 Jean-Yves Leloup, *The Gospel of Thomas*, trans. Joseph Rowe (Rochester, VT: Inner Traditions, 2005), Logion 12, 84. Translated from the Coptic by Jean-Yves Leloup.

80 *The Didache: Text, Translation, Analysis and Commentary* (Collegeville, MN: Liturgical Press, 2003). Translated and edited by Aaron Milavec.

81 Matthew Fox, *The Coming of the Cosmic Christ* (San Francisco: Harper, 1988), 161.

82 Victor E. Frankl, MD, PhD, *Man's Search for Ultimate Meaning* (New York: Basic Books, 2000), 148. The quote is from the "Father of Ethology," Konrad Lorenz.

83 Ludwig Feuerbach, *The Essence of Christianity* (New York: Harper & Row, 1957), 29 ff. Translated from the German by George Eliot (Marian Evans).

84 Stephen P. Garvey, *Beyond Repair? America's Death Penalty* (Durham, NC: Duke University Press, 2003), 33–34.

85 Dominique J.-F. de Quervain, et al., "The Neural Basis for Altruistic Punishment," *Science* 305, August 27, 2004.

86 Josiah Rich, MD, et al., "Medicine and the Epidemic of Incarceration in the United States," *New England Journal of Medicine*, June 2, 2011.

87 Franz Alt, *Frieden Ist Moeglich. Die Politik Der Bergpredigt* (Muenchen Zurich: R. Piper Verlag, 1983).

88 Leo Tolstoy, *The Kingdom of God Is Within You*, trans. Constance Garnett (La Vergne, TN: Wildside Press, 2006).

89 Philip Yancey, *Where Is God When It Hurts?* (Grand Rapids, MI: Zondervan, 1977), 246.

90 Stephen G. Post, *Unlimited Love. Altruism, Compassion and Service* (2003), 96.

91 Stephen J. Pope, *The Evolution of Altruism and the Ordering of Love* (Washington, DC: Georgetown University Press, 2007).

92 John Sellars, *Stoicism* (Berkeley: University of California Press, 2006), 131.

93 *The Cambridge Dictionary of Philosophy*, 460 and 298 resp.

94 Matthew Fox, *The Coming of the Cosmic Christ* (San Francisco: Harper, 1988), 163 ff.

95 *The Complete Dictionary of Symbols* (San Francisco: Chronicle Books, 2005), 445.

96 *A New Catholic Commentary on the Holy Scripture* (Nashville: Thomas Nelson, 1969), 180. Old Testament editor: Rev. Leonard Johnston, STL, LSS.

97 www.animal-symbols.com/snake-symbol.html.

98 Pope John Paul I, http:/www.ewtn.com/library/papaldoc/jp2tb26.htm.

99 Leo Tolstoy, *Collected Works (Russian Edition)*, Vol. 12 (Moscow: Khudozhestvennaya Literatura, 1964), 218 ff.

100 Nicolai Berdyaev, *Dukh I Real'nost' (Spirit and Reality)* (Moscow: Astrel, 2011), 272.

101 *The Hindu Tradition* (New York: Modern Library, 1966), 84 ff.

102 Robert W. Funk, *The Five Gospels: What Did Jesus Really Say?* (New York: Harper One, 1997), 464. Coauthored by Roy W. Hoover and the Jesus Seminar.

103 The Gospel According to Luke 16:19–31. Luke is unique in considering wealth not an impediment to salvation but a sin

to be punished and misery a virtue to be rewarded. The story stands alone without a connection to the preceding or following text and is not even introduced by the words *Jesus said*. Therefore I believe that it is more representative of Luke's views than those of Jesus.

[104] Victor Frankl, MD, PhD, *Man's Search for Ultimate Meaning* (New York: Basic Books, 2000), 123.

[105] Seneca, "Moral Letters to Lucilius/Letter 96" http://en.wikisource.org/wiki/Moral_letters_to_Lucilius/Letter_96.

[106] Matthew Fox, *The Coming of the Cosmic Christ* (San Francisco: Harper, 1988), 222.

[107] William Shakespeare, *Hamlet,* Act 3, Scene 1

[108] *A New Catholic Commentary on the Holy Scripture,* paragraph 742a, 951; paragraph 762n, 983 ff; paragraph 818g, 1071 ff.

[109] *The Complete Dictionary of Symbols,* 513 ff.

[110] Helen Bergen, "Living One's Truth," www.vatican.va/roman_curia/pontifical_councils/interelg/documents/rc_pc_interelg_doc_20030203_new-age_en.htlm. Published in *The Furrow* January 2000, cited in the Vatican publication "Jesus Christ the Bearer of the Water of Life."

[111] "Sabra and Shatilla," http://jewishvoiceforpeace.org/content/sabra-and-shatilla.

[112] Ward Churchill, *A Little Matter of Genocide* (San Francisco: City Lights Books, 1997), 139 (quoted in Ashburn *The Ranks of Death,* op. cit. 19).

[113] Ibid., 172 (quoted from Bradford *of Plymouth Plantation,* op. cit. 296).

[114] *The Didache: Text, Translation, Analysis and Commentary,* 110.

[115] Ibid., 3 ff.

[116] Arthur Cushman McGiffert, *The Apostles' Creed* (New York: Charles Scribner's Sons, 1902), 10.

[117] *Encyclopaedia Britannica* (Chicago: William Benton, 1972), Volume 6, 385. Found under the heading "Constantine."

[118] John Mark Mattox, *Saint Augustine and the Theory of War* (New York: Continuum, 2006), 47.

[119] Ibid., 46.

[120] Ibid., 48.

[121] "'American Sniper' Killed at Gun Range," by Matt Pearce and Molly Hennessy-Fiske, *Los Angeles Times,* February 4, 2013, A5.

[122] Tolstoy, *Collected Works (Russian Edition),* 218 ff. I fully agree with the statement quoted here as much as I disagree with the one quoted under citation 99.

[123] Meister Eckhart, *Deutsche Predigten und Traktate.* Translated into modern German from Middle High German by Joseph Quint (Zurch: Diogenes Verlag A. G., 1979), Predigt 1, "Intravit Jesus in templum ..." p. 153 ff.

[124] Attar, "Rabi'a: Her Words and Life in 'Memorial of the Friends of God,'" in *Early Islamic Mysticism,* ed. Michael A. Sells (New York: Paulist Press, 1996), 151.

[125] Nikolai Berdyaev, *Dukh I Realnost' (Spirit and Reality)* Moscow: Astrel, 2011), 336.

[126] Theodor Herzl Gaster, *Passover, Its History and Traditions* (New York: Henry Schuman, 1949), 93 ff.
Similar interpretations may be found on the following websites:
http://chabad.org/therbebbe/letters/default cdo/aid/1925111/jewish/Passover-The-Meaning-of-True-Freedom.htm
www.gatherthejews.com/2011/04/passover-and-the-true-meaning-of-freedom/
www.haaretz.com/jewish-world/rabbis-round-table/happiness-in-slavery-the-true-meaning-of-passover-1.511912

[127] Rabbi Nathaniel Laufer, *Leading the Passover Journey* (Woodstock, VT: Jewish Lights, 2005), 130.

[128] *The Complete Dictionary of Symbols*, 130.

[129] Jean-Yves Leloup, *The Gospel of Philip*, trans. Joseph Rowe (from the French) (Rochester, VT: Inner Traditions, 2004), 53, plate 104. Translated from the Coptic by Jean-Yves Leloup.

[130] Ibid., 121, plate 121.

[131] Ludwig Feuerbach, *Thoughts on Death and Immortality*, trans. James A. Massey (Berkeley: University of California Press,1980), 126.

[132] Joseph Cardinal Ratzinger, *Introduction to Christianity* (San Francisco: Ignatius Press, 1990), 172 ff.

[133] Abraham Cohen, *Everyone's Talmud* (New York: Schocken Books, 1949), 96.

[134] *Catholic Encyclopedia,* www.newadvent.org/cathen/15764c.htm.

[135] Matthew Fox, *Original Blessing* (New York: Jeremy P. Thatcher/ Putnam, 2000), 49.

[136] Josephus, "The Antiquities of the Jews," in *The Works of Josephus* (Peabody, MA: Hendrickson, 1987), chapter 5, section 2, 484.

[137] Ibid.

[138] Roger Haight SJ, *Jesus Symbol of God* (Maryknoll, NY: Orbis Books, 1999), 463 ff.

[139] Ibid., 428.

[140] Ibid., 295.

[141] Ibid., appendix, 510 and 513.

[142] Kersey Graves, *The World's Sixteen Crucified Saviors or Christianity before Christ* (Kila, MT: Kessinger Publishing Company. Originally published in 1875, year of cited reprint not given).

[143] Fulton J. Sheen, *The Seven Last Words* (New York: Society of St. Paul, 1996), 58.

[144] "Liturgy of the Hours" www.ebreviary.com.

[145] "The Mind of Mahatma Gandhi," www.mkgandhi.org/ momgandhi/chap18.htm.

[146] Francis B. Randall, "Introduction. Marx the Romantic," in *The Communist Manifesto by Karl Marx and Friedrich Engels*, ed. Joseph Katz (New York: Pocket Books, 1964), 20.

[147] Bertrand Russell, *A History of Weatern Philosophy* (New York: Simon and Schuster, 1972),364.

[148] Kenneth R. Weiss, "Runaway Population Growth Often Fuels Youth-Driven Uprisings," *Los Angeles Times*, July 22, 2012.

[149] John B. Noss, *Man's Religions,* 6th ed. (New York: Macmillan and Collier McMillan, 1980), 513.

[150] Jonathan Riley-Smith, *The Crusades* (New York: Continuum, 2005), 17 ff.

[151] Edmond Burke, *Reflections on the French Revolution* (Cambridge, England: Cambridge University Press, 1929), 62 ff.

[152] Jeremy Bentham, *Theory of Legislation*, trans. from the French of Etienne Dumont by R. Hildreth, Vol. I (Boston: Weeks, Jordan, 1840), 110.

[153] Jeremy Bentham, *The Principles of Moral and Legislation* (Amherst, NY: Prometheus Books, 1988), 2.

[154] Thomas Paine, *Rights of Man* (Mineola, NY: Dover, 1999), 65 ff.

[155] J. B. S. Haldane, FRS, *The Inequality of Man* (Harmondsworth Middlesex, England: Penguin, 1937).

[156] *A New Catholic Commentary on the Holy Scripture*, 1013, paragraph 784b.

[157] Jean-Ives Leloup, *The Gospel of Thomas*, Logion 3, 9 and 67. Translated from the Coptic by Jean-Yves Leloup.

[158] Ibid., Logion 113, 57 and 220.

[159] Joseph A. Bracken, SJ, *Christianity and Process Thought* (Philadelphia: Templeton Foundation Press, 2006), 55.

[160] Ibid., 57.

[161] Alfred North Whitehead, *Process and Reality*, corrected edition (New york: Free Press, 1985), 349 ff.

162 John B. Cobb Jr., *Christ in a Pluralistic Age* (Eugene, OR: Wipf and Stock, 1998), 221 ff.

163 Pierre Teilhard de Chardin, *Le Phenomene Humain* (Paris: Editions du Seuil, 1955), 291.

164 Pierre Teilhard de Chardin, *Le Milieu Divin* (Paris: Editions du Seuil, 1957), 145.

165 Ibid., 124.

166 Gustavo Gutierrez, *A Theology of Liberation*, trans. Sister Caridad Inda and John Eagleson (Maryknoll, New York: Orbis Books, 1988), 10 ff. Citation is from "Catolicos holandeses" 29.

167 John B. Cobb Jr., *Christ in a Pluralistic Age*, (Eugene, OR: Wipf and Stock, 1998), 228.

168 Richard Maurice Bucke, MD, *Cosmic Consciousness* (New Hyde Park, NY: University Books, 1961), 86.

169 Jean-Ives Leloup, *The Gospel of Thomas*, Logion 54, 33 and 149.

170 S. G. F. Brandon, "The Death of James the Just, a New Interpretation," in *Studies in Mysticism and Religion* (Jerusalem: Magnus Press, 1967), cited by Reza Aslan, 268.

171 Reza Aslan, *Zealot* (New York: Random House, 2013), 127 ff.

172 *A New Catholic Commentary on the Holy Scripture*, Paragraph 710c, 903.

173 Meister Eckhart, *Deutsche Predigten und Traktate*. Translated into modern German from Middle High German by Joseph Quint. (Zurich: Diogenes Verlag A.G., 1979), Predigt 32, "Beati paupers spiritu ..." 303 ff.

174 Ibid., 307.

175 Matthew Fox, *Breakthrough, Meister Eckharts Creation Spirituality in New Translation* (Garden City, NY: Image Books, 1980), 213.

176 Meister Eckhart, *Deutsche Predigten und Traktate*. Translated into modern German from Middle High German by Joseph

Quint. (Zurich: Diogenes Verlag A.G., 1979). Predigt 46, "Beati qui esuriunt et sitiunt justiciam," 370.

[177] Ibid., 371.

[178] Jennifer Ross, "Torah Class," www.torahclass.com/archived-articles/429-anav-by-jennifer-ross.

[179] Martin Buber, *Ich Und Du* (Heidelberg, Germany: Verlag Lambert Schneider, 1983), 42.

[180] *The Cambridge Dictionary of Philosophy*, 318.

[181] David Steinberg, "Where Is Your Heart? Some Body Part Metaphors and Euphemisms in Biblical Hebrew," www.adath-shalom.ca/body_metaphors_bib_hebrew.htm.

[182] Richard Maurice Bucke, MD, *Cosmic Consciousness* (New Hyde Park, NY: University Books, 1961), 270

[183] Ibid., 274.

[184] Fyodor Dostoyevsky, *Besy (Demons)* in *Collected Works*, Volume 7. (Moscow: Gosudarstvennoye Izdatel'stvo Khudozhestvennoy Literatury, 1957), 614.

[185] W. Somerset Maugham, *The Razor's Edge*, (New York: Penguin, 1992), 275 ff.

[186] Anthony Curtis, "Introduction," in *The Razor's Edge* by Somerset Maugham (New York: Penguin, 1992), XVI ff.

[187] Jose Ortega y Gasset, *Meditaciones De Quijote* (Madrid, Spain: Catedra, Letras Hispanicas, 2012), 77.

[188] Ibid., footnote, 82.

[189] Jean-Yves Leloup, *The Gospel of Thomas*, trans. Joseph Rowe (Rochester, VT: Inner Traditions 2005), 33 and 153, Logion 58. Translation from the Coptic and commentary by Jean-Yves Leloup.

[190] Father John-Julian, OJN, *The Complete Julian of Norwich* (Brewster, MA: Paraclete, 2009), 146 ff. and 408 ff.

[191] Richard Maurice Bucke, MD, *Cosmic Consciousness* (New Hyde Park NY: University Books, 1961). 62.

[192] Tom Kington and Henry Chu, "Pope Seeks to Shift Catholic Church's Priority from Dogma to Mercy," *Los Angeles Times,* September 19, 2013.

[193] Monica Sjöö and Barbara Mor, *The Great Cosmic Mother* (New York: Harper One, 1991), 49.

[194] Vanamali, *Shakti: Realm of the Divine Mother* (Rochester, VT: Inner Traditions, 2008), 4 ff.

[195] Dr. Martin Luther, *Der Kleine Katechismus* (Fechenheim, Germany: Allg. Pfarrwitwenkasse als Verlegerin bei Maindruck, 1946), 107.

[196] Josh McDowell, *New Evidence That Demands a Verdict* (Nashville, TN: Thomas Nelson, 1999).

[197] Feuerbach, *Thoughts on Death and Immortality*, 123.

[198] *A New Catholic Commentary on the Holy Scripture*, paragraph 718h, 916.

[199] *The Didache: Text, Translation, Analysis and Commentary*, 109.

INDEX

TRUE DIRECTIONS
An affiliate of Tarcher Books

OUR MISSION

Tarcher's mission has always been to publish books
that contain great ideas. Why? Because:

GREAT LIVES BEGIN WITH GREAT IDEAS

At Tarcher, we recognize that many talented authors, speakers,
educators, and thought-leaders share this mission and deserve to be
published – many more than Tarcher can reasonably publish ourselves.
True Directions is ideal for authors and books that increase awareness,
raise consciousness, and inspire others to live their ideals and passions.

Like Tarcher, True Directions books are designed to do three things:
inspire, inform, and motivate.

Thus, True Directions is an ideal way for these important voices
to bring their messages of hope, healing, and help to the world.

Every book published by True Directions– whether it is non-
fiction, memoir, novel, poetry or children's book – continues
Tarcher's mission to publish works that bring positive change
in the world. We invite you to join our mission.

For more information, see the True Directions website:
www.iUniverse.com/TrueDirections/SignUp

Be a part of Tarcher's community to bring positive change in this world!
See exclusive author videos, discover new and exciting books, learn about
upcoming events, connect with author blogs and websites, and more!
www.tarcherbooks.com

TRUE DIRECTIONS
AN AFFILIATE OF TARCHER BOOKS